Momvotional

365 Days of Motivation, Positivity &
Self Care Tips for Every Mother

SEULETYM

~ Copyright, Disclaimer & Legal ~

~ *Dedication* ~

*This book is dedicated to the tired,
overwhelmed, stressed out, lonely,
exhausted, frustrated mother who is in need
of a sprinkle of daily positivity, motivation
and inspiration to keep them going. This
book is also dedicated to expectant mothers
to get them prepared for the journey ahead.*

*I hope you will enjoy reading this book as
much as I've enjoyed writing it.*

*With love from one mother trying to figure
it out to the other..*

Denise.xx

TABLE OF CONTENTS

~ Part 1 - Tips for Staying Motivated & Self Care ~

Motherhood is one of those journeys we go through without a manual, guide or direction on how things would turn out. Unfortunately this can lead to demotivation in mothers who are constantly left feeling burnt out with nowhere to really turn to.

Additionally we spend so much time looking after our little ones and everyone else that we end up neglecting ourselves.

So in the next few days, we are going to be exploring some tips that can help you stay motivated as well as take better care of yourself. Because at the end of the day if mama ain't happy, then the children really can't be.

January

January 1
It all Starts From Within

Hey mama, as you begin this first day of the new year, I want you to step into it with a positive mindset. Because the way you think can determine how you feel and act. So today I want you to make this promise to yourself. Even better, note it down somewhere to serve as a reminder as you go through this new year.

"It's going to be an amazing year and I'm going to be the best mother I can be"

January 2
Push Yourself Today

Feeling a little low? Try to push yourself today mama because no one else is going to do it for you. Remember those precious little ones are relying on you, so keep pushing and don't give up.

January 3
Focus on YOU

As mothers, we spend so much time caring for everyone else that we forget about ourselves. So today I urge you to think about one thing that makes you feel really good - apart from your kids, husband, and everything else that you surround yourself with on a daily basis. I'm referring to those fun things that you used to enjoy prior to having children like doing your nails, getting a haircut, shopping, going to the movies, etc.

Now promise yourself that you will find at least one day this week/month to do one of those fun things. This is a great way to forget about everything else and focus on you for a little minute. And this can do wonders to your sanity.

January 4
Take a Deep Breath

Having one of those days where it feels like you are going crazy? Now I want you to take a few minutes today and go somewhere quiet and alone. Even if it means locking yourself up in the bathroom away from the kids for 5 minutes (just make sure the kids are safe of course). Avoid your phone or any distractions. Close your eyes, take 10 deep breaths in through the nose and out through the mouth, and notice how much of a difference it will make.

January 5
One Step at a Time

Just because we can do it all as mothers doesn't mean we always have to do it all. Today I want you to concentrate on one thing at a time. If you think about everything you have to do, then your energy levels will feel even lower.

Take the day one step at a time and don't focus on what you have left to do. When you only focus on the immediate action, you won't mentally deplete what energy you have left.

January 6
Self Compassion is Key

Overworked and Underappreciated - that pretty much sums up the life of a mother. Everyone else gets their needs met by mama except mama herself. So today I want you to take some time to practice some self compassion. Give yourself the same love you give to your children, spouse and everyone else around you. Treat yourself with care and kindness even if it means eating something healthy, having a nice bath, pampering yourself, getting your nails done or just listening to some relaxing music to keep you calm. Whatever you do, be kind to yourself today.

January 7
Remember Your Accomplishments

Sometimes it may seem like you aren't where you want to be right now. But one thing you need to remind yourself is that you are no longer where you used to be.

Being alive and seeing another day is a huge accomplishment, pushing out that child is a huge accomplishment, raising a child is a huge accomplishment and putting others' needs before yours are all accomplishments you need to be proud of. Remember that, give yourself a pat on the back and celebrate yourself.

January 8
Positive Affirmation of the Day

Today is a day of positive affirmation. As you go through this day, repeat these words to yourself each time you find yourself drifting apart or feeling a little low.

"I am immensely grateful for my wonderful life. I am grateful for my beautiful child who has made me happy and made my life worth living".

January 9
It's OK to Make Mistakes

It's ok to mistake a baby's hunger for being tired, or colic for a wet nappy. Don't fret over it and think that you have to get it right all the time or else something bad is going to happen. Most mistakes are forgivable when you are trying something new - especially as a mother having to figure things out and learn on the job.

Mistakes can and should be considered learning tools that enable you to learn more about yourself. Instead use that as an opportunity to gain new skills and experience, that will essentially help you move closer to achieving your best potential as a mother.

January 10
Filter Away Negativity

There's nothing worse than starting your day with negative thoughts. Before you start your day, be sure to filter the negative thoughts out of your mind and focus on the positive things that make you happy. Tell yourself today will be great and nothing will come in the way of your happiness. This will allow you to begin to focus on what matters. Unless you cleanse your mind of poisonous thoughts, you will find it impossible to think clearly and believe in yourself.

January 11
It's OK to Cry it Out

Sometimes, it may seem like nothing is working out and all you want to do is let it all out. Most people mistake crying for being a weakness when it can actually be a good thing.

Research has found that in addition to being self-soothing, shedding emotional tears releases oxytocin and endorphins. These chemicals make people feel good and may also ease both physical and emotional pain. In this way, crying can help reduce pain and promote a sense of well-being. So if it means locking yourself up in the bathroom and letting it all out - go for it mama, it will do you some good.

January 12
Look at the Bigger Picture

Having one of those days where it seems difficult or impossible to do anything? If you have difficulty starting tasks or you lose your motivation, stop what you're doing, take a deep breath and focus on your end goal.

Remember why you are raising those beautiful child(ren) and how much they will grow to love you and care for you when you are old and grey. Look at the bigger picture, appreciate where you are right now and enjoy the moment.

January 13
Celebrate Every Win

Don't underestimate those precious little accomplishments like finally settling a fussy baby, or making it through another hectic day. Praising yourself for the small things that you've accomplished will help motivate you and keep you on the right path to reaching your goals. While it might seem silly, it really can be a great motivator, especially when you're lacking the energy and drive to get through the day.

January 14
Don't be Hard on Yourself

Don't be hard on yourself today. The fact that you are trying your best right now is a sign of how strong you are. You don't need to have it all figured out. Nobody in this world has it all figured out at the end of the day.

January 15
Yes You Can Do It

To effectively push yourself forward and embrace challenges, you have to develop a can-do attitude. Doing this requires a commitment to yourself that you will do whatever it takes to become more disciplined and that you will strive for what matters most to you despite all odds. So be strong today mama and believe you can do whatever life throws at you.

January 16
Break Those Bad Habits

We all have those bad habits that prevent us from achieving the things we really and truly deserve. A very unconscious bad habit that most mothers have is failing to look after our physical, mental and emotional well being. We tend to worry about everyone else but ourselves.

You need to get rid of all the bad habits that keep you from being the best version of yourself. Your habits shape your life, so if you want to build a good, meaningful and happier life, you need to work on eliminating the bad habits that keep you from the true happiness you deserve.

January 17
It's a Learning Experience

Whether you are dealing with a toddler's tantrums or struggling to get a fussy baby to eat, remember every experience that you go through, be it good or bad, should be seen as a learning experience.

If you are struggling with something or feel you made a mistake, don't regret it and don't feel bad about making it. Instead, focus on what you can do to improve things. Accept each challenge and obstacle happily and wholeheartedly rather than seeing them as setbacks in your life.

January 18
Feeling the Guilt?

Mom guilt is one of the biggest problems we experience as mothers. This could range anywhere from the feeling of guilt of missing out on your kids growing up because you have to go back to work, not feeding them enough healthy meals, or not involving them in enough activities.

Remember there is no such thing as the perfect mother and we just have to live and learn on the job. So don't be too hard on yourself, and if it's something that is consuming you, then find alternative ways to deal with the situation at hand rather than worrying yourself over it.

January 19
Take a Step Back

Many mothers tend to jump right into their day without thinking it through. They have a list of chores in their mind and are planning on when they can complete which chore. However, without fail, something always gets forgotten.

To keep this from happening to you, take a deep breath when you first wake up and take a step back from your busy mind. Take the time to write down your tasks so you have an idea of how much time each one will take so you can more effectively plan how you will tackle the list.

January 20
Positive Affirmation of the Day

Today is a day of positive affirmation. As you go through this day, repeat these words to yourself each time you find yourself drifting apart or feeling a little low.

"I am grateful for every moment I spend with my children every day because I know that it will never return".

January 21
Prepare for the Unexpected

Being a mother means living a life of uncertainty. From a child suddenly running a temperature in the middle of night and you having to take them to a hospital, to a clingy baby who won't let mama do anything.

As much as you may have the best laid out plans, it never fails that something will happen that ruins those plans.

So remember to make exceptions in your schedule for things that might come up that you hadn't planned for. Accept that things aren't always going to go as planned and prepare yourself mentally for it so it doesn't come to you as a shock.

January 22
You are A Superwoman

You may not feel like you've got it together, but in the eyes of your little one(s), you are nothing but a superwoman. Always remember that each time you feel a little down and be incredibly proud of yourself.

January 23
Don't take it Personal

As a mother, it's very easy to take things personally when they don't go as planned. And sometimes this can even make you feel like a failure. Remember you are raising another human with their own feelings and emotions and cannot always determine how they will react. Don't take things that happen personally, because a lot of things are beyond our control. It isn't your fault. We have no control over what happens to us, but can certainly control our emotions and how we react to things.

January 24
See the Good in Everything

Life is too short to live in misery and blame everything on your problems. Never blame, complain or take things personally. Instead, focus on the more important things in your life, those things that you are grateful for like your kids, being alive, being healthy and having food to eat.

January 25
Find Your Mantra

A mantra doesn't have to be long; it just has to get you excited. Here are some examples;

"I am beautiful, "I am doing an amazing job", " I am an awesome mother", "I am a superwoman".

When you lack energy and feel unmotivated, repeat your words of mantra to yourself to remind you what matters the most and keep you going.

January 26
It Gets Better with Time

When you start a new job, it takes time to become fully competent on the job. When you learn how to drive, it takes time and practice to become a fully competent driver. Athletes practice every single day to win the race. And even at that, we still learn as we go.

Being a mother isn't any different. Everyday is a new learning experience and as overwhelming as it may seem, it gets better with time and practice. So stay calm, enjoy the process and don't try to figure everything out in one day.

January 27
Don't Let the Obstacles Get You

Life is full of obstacles and challenges. And being a mother doesn't come with any exceptions. If you allow these things to stand in your way, you will never succeed in achieving anything. When you face challenges in life, you have to find a way to face them head on and make it through the fire and to the other side.

January 28
Be Open to Change

Change can be difficult for everyone, especially with mothers. From dealing with changes to your body after childbirth, to losing the identity of who you used to be prior to having children. However, the more open to change that you are, the easier the transition will be when you are ready to make changes in your life.

There will come a point in your life where things will need to change in order for you to move forward. Don't fight it, embrace it and continue moving forward despite how challenging it may seem now. Afterall staying in the same place all your life eventually gets boring.

January 29
Avoid Perfectionist Syndrome

House looking a mess? Laundry not done in a week? Don't have the energy to cook? So what? That doesn't make you a bad mother. Yes a clean house is good, however this doesn't mean your house is always going to be spotless 24/7. You have kids now, remember! That laundry can wait till later, I'm sure the kids have something to wear until then. Plus ordering a takeaway instead of making your own homemade pizza from scratch isn't going to send you to mother jail. So don't be hard on yourself - life itself isn't perfect and neither are you.

January 30
Stop Overthinking

Overthinking is a thief of joy and only makes things worse than they actually are. So if you find yourself overthinking things, take a step back, take a few deep breaths and accept that what's meant to be would be.

January 31
Set Some Self Care Goals

As we step into a new month, there's nothing better than setting goals for the month ahead. Goals are an important part of our everyday life and will help you find the motivation to keep going.

So remember to set some self care goals for yourself next month, Whether it be treating yourself to a spa, getting those nails done, joining a dance class, getting your hair done or even catching up with friends, write those goals down and work towards achieving them next month.

February

February 1
Can You Feel the Love?

Hey mama, welcome to the new month of love. As you begin this new month, I want you to step into it with a positive mindset. So today I want you to make this promise to yourself.

" I'm going to love on myself this month even if no one else does"

Remember those words as you go through this month and affirm those words each time you are feeling a little low.

February 2
Listen to Advice

Take the advice that is worth listening to and make it a part of your goal. Don't think that you know everything. Allow yourself the vulnerability to know when you need to take advice or let the advice go.

February 3
Don't Dwell on It

Looking and feeling like a mess? Not had a shower in days? House looking a little untidy? Those legs due for a shave? Nails looking a little crusty? Welcome to motherhood! It's so easy to look at what's in-front of us right now and feel dreadful about it all.

But one thing you must remember is that it isn't always going to be that way and this is only temporary. A time will come when the kids will grow up, become independent, and you will have all the time in the world to focus on you. This however doesn't mean you should completely neglect yourself right now, it just means you shouldn't sweat it if things don't look as perfect as you would wish for right now.

February 4
Bin the Negativity

Feeling negative today? Honestly it's only human to feel that way sometimes. But what's the point of dwelling on negativity? What difference would that realistically make on what you are going through right now? You have two choices; stay feeling negative or you could invest that same energy into getting yourself out of the funk.

February 5
Be Happy

Happiness is not having what you want but appreciating what you already have. We spend so much time chasing rainbows and unicorns that we forget the incredible things we have right in front of us. Don't let the pursuit of what you want prevent you from enjoying the happiness you have right in front of you.

February 6
Don't Work Yourself Up

Can't figure out why your baby won't stop crying? Did you give them paracetamol thinking they were teething whereas they were really struggling with colic? Feeling like a big failure because you made a parenting mistake? Well don't we all make mistakes?

Especially as a mother dealing with a baby who can only express themselves through crying. As long as your child is happy and healthy, you are doing amazing. Don't work yourself up, instead use this as a learning experience to do better next time.

February 7
Look After Yourself First

And this doesn't mean being selfish or neglecting your child. It simply means don't forget to take care of yourself. Think of it this way, if you are feeling drained, exhausted and tired, then where would you find the strength to look after your kids?

So remember to eat something healthy, do some yoga, read a book, meditate, pray or do anything that can help you recharge and reenergize so you are able to look after your little ones too.

February 8
A Gentle Reminder

Today I just want you to remember this;

"You got this mama"

February 9
Step Up the Challenge

Scared of that challenge? Well we never learn by staying inside our comfort zone. When you make it a priority to step outside that comfort zone, incredible things will begin to happen. So whatever challenge you are facing right now, just remember it's an opportunity for you to level up to bigger things.

February 10
Be Proud of Yourself

Can't seem to figure things out? Stop doubting yourself and your abilities as a mother. You should be proud of every single day you spend raising that child. And as long as your child is breathing, happy and healthy, you have absolutely nothing to worry about.

February 11
Start the Day Right

When you're starting your day, try to never start it on a bad note. This could involve doing any of your favorite things like having a shower, listening to music or having a warm cup of espresso to kick start your day.

Some people read a book while their mind is fresh and others start with meditation. Typically, if your day commences well, then the rest of the day doesn't seem so menacing and you can better handle situations you face through the morning, afternoon, evening and night.

February 12
Be Thankful

We spend so much time not valuing the amazing things we have in front of us. Make a list of all the things you can't live without. These are the things you must be thankful for. Every night, go to sleep right after you read through the list, remembering all the things you have and should appreciate.

February 13
Keep Your Spirits High

In the daytime when the sun shines on your path, you can surely find something to keep your mind active and occupied with optimistic thoughts. Stay light on your feet and enjoy the great moments you have experienced again and again to keep your spirits high.

February 14
Soak into the Love Today

Happy Valentine's Day to you mama - a special day of love and affection. Today should be a reminder of how much love you have around you be it from your partner, kids, family or even yourself.

Look around you and see all the love you are surrounded by and take time to appreciate it. And even if you feel like there isn't enough love around you, go love yourself beautifully. Because at the end of the day no one is ever going to love you as much as you love YOU. Plus enjoy that chocolate and glass of wine, and do not apologize for it.

February 15
Comparison is the Thief of Joy

The people you surround yourself with have a tremendous impact on your mind. As mothers it's very easy to fall into the trap of comparing yourself to other mothers. From the mom whose kid is so well behaved in public whilst your kid is throwing the biggest tantrum, to the mom whose kid sleeps throughout the night while you are still struggling to get a straight 3 hours sleep every night.

If you spend all your time comparing yourself with others, you will never give yourself room to appreciate your own abilities. So take a step back and appreciate what you have. Understand that every child is different.

February 16
You are a Superwoman

Today I want you to appreciate yourself. Be proud of how far you've come and all the battles you've been dealing with so far - *you know those silent tears in the bathroom and sleepless nights.* Pat yourself in the back and celebrate your incredible strength and achievements because you are a superwoman.

February 17
Learn to Deal with It

Life is often full of setbacks and this isn't any different with motherhood. Therefore you should learn to deal with adversity and setbacks during a new challenge or activity. By dealing with these you will learn the skills and attributes needed to handle more challenging setbacks in life.

February 18
Be Content with Yourself

We all know how incredibly easy it is to beat ourselves up especially when things don't go as planned. However, doing so only reinforces negative thought patterns and slows us down. It's okay to go at your own pace. As long as you are steadily working toward your goals, you are on the path you need to be!

February 19
Today is a Blessing

Everyday is a blessing. No new day is guaranteed. If you are alive reading this, you are luckier than some who didn't make it to see today. Every new day is a new opportunity to try something new, seize it!

February 20
Lead with Positivity

The positive things you do for yourself can leave a lasting impression in the life of a loved one. Especially as mothers, our kids are like sponges and our habits can be easily grabbed by them.

Remember that we change the world not by pointing the finger, but by changing ourselves.

Likewise our kids will see and emulate the positive changes we make. The more positive you become, the more positivity you give to a world that desperately needs it.

February 21
It's Ok to be Selfish

Remember that it's all about you . At the end of the day, it's easy to attend to everybody's needs except ourselves, especially as mothers. Sure it's good to be selfless, but not at the expense of our own lives. By focusing on yourself first, you put yourself in the healthy position to eventually help others without enabling. So take time to just focus on YOU sometimes.

February 22
Try Something New

Sometimes the monotony of life is overwhelming. We cope with this through recreation and hobbies alike. Every now and then it's good to throw a new hobby into the mix. You'll thank yourself after giving that one activity you've been wanting to try for years a chance.

It doesn't hurt to try! Think about a new activity that you love and indulge in it for a change. By putting yourself into new situations, you never know what opportunities you open yourself up to and how much progress you can make along the way.

February 23
You Can Do It

Hey mama, remember that nobody else can do what you need to do for yourself. The only person that needs to take action in the equation is you. And that is something you are capable of!

February 24
Enjoy the Present

As mothers we spend time planning for our future and that of the kids that we sometimes forget to enjoy the moment. You're tarnishing the present if you consistently dwell in the past. With that said, it is also important to not be so consumed by the future that we are unable to enjoy the present.

Bring yourself back to reality every so often if you have to. Focusing on your goals is great, but losing sight of how special the now is can be unfortunate.

February 25
Get Yourself Back Up

As you try to go through your incredible journey of motherhood, you are going to experience some pitfalls along the way. Remember that this experience is not exclusive to you and it's nothing personal. However when you do fall, the most important thing is to get yourself back up again.

February 26
A Quick Note to Yourself

Hey mama, I want you to remind yourself of these words today.

"I am confident"
"I am beautiful"
"I am unstoppable"

February 27
You are Doing Amazing

Hey mama, guess what? You are doing amazing. I know you've heard this before but this is just a gentle reminder in case you find yourself drifting apart. Tell yourself you are doing amazing and see just how amazing today turns out to be.

February 28
Be Happy Where You Are

Wherever you are in life right now, it's okay. It's exactly where you were supposed to be. It's better to acknowledge where you find yourself, than be in denial.

Accept your place for what it is because it's all a part of your journey in life. Feeling terrible about things or judging yourself can only bring you down. So keep your head up, stay positive and be grateful for where you are.

February 29
Positive Affirmation of the Day

Today is a day of positive affirmation. As you go through this day, repeat these words to yourself each time you find yourself drifting apart or feeling a little low.

"Every minute I appreciate the completeness of my journey and I am aware that by appreciating the completeness of my journey I realize greater happiness, peace, and joy".

March

March 1
Keep Marching On

Hey mama, welcome to another new month. As you begin this new month, I want you to step into it with a positive mindset. Because the way you think can impact how you feel. So today I want you to make this promise to yourself.

"I would not let anything beyond my control overwhelm me"

Remember those words as you go through this month and remind yourself of that each time you are feeling a little low.

March 2
Go at Your Own Pace

We all know how incredibly easy it is to beat ourselves up. However, doing so only reinforces negative thought patterns and slows us down.

If your child isn't ready to be potty trained, don't force them to because your friend's child of a similar age is already getting potty trained.

It's okay to go at your own pace and don't feel the need to do things because someone else is doing it. Your child is probably better at something else than the next child.

March 3
Never Ever Quit

No matter how tough things may seem, don't you ever quit! There's a champion in all of us that is waiting to be discovered. Many of us have never gotten in touch with the winner inside. That's okay, it doesn't mean you cannot build a relationship with the best you today! Your best inner you is extending their hand so go grab it.

March 4
Do it for You

A little healthy competition is fine. But when you become consumed by the desire to do better than others you cross over into unhealthy territory. In other words, if you're trying to do things with the goal of impressing others, then your priorities are misplaced. So whatever you do, make sure you are keeping focused on yourself, you deserve it.

March 5
Get the Lights In

One way to start your day off right is to get some light exposure. The first thing that you should do in the morning is open your blinds and curtains to allow more natural light to flow into your room.

Your body is programmed to wake up to natural light. If it is during the winter and it's dark in the mornings where you live, then you may want to look into some artificial lights. There are special lights that you can buy, called "*happy light*" that simulates natural light. So, while you are doing other things, like gathering your clothing or making meals, keep exposing yourself to the natural light, it would do good to your mental health.

March 6
Avoid Comparison

Never ever see the need to compare yourself to other mothers. The path you're on is unique to you. By comparing yourself to others, you not only begin to worry, but you slow yourself down. The last thing you need is distraction from your own journey.

March 7
Struggles are Necessary

Struggles are a natural part of life. Afterall what would life be without a few struggles here and there right? The same applies to being a mother. You will never go through that journey smoothly or without any struggles. Remember a good mother isn't one that never struggled, but the one that never gave up despite the struggles. So trust the process and enjoy this incredible phase of life.

March 8
Spoil Yourself Today

And spoiling yourself doesn't mean you have to splurge on the most expensive thing to feel good. Something so little like buying a new dress, shoes, purse for yourself or getting your hair and nails done can do just the trick.

Afterall we spoil our little ones all the time with toys, love etc, so why not add yourself to that equation.

March 9
Visualization is Powerful

If you're feeling your motivation levels waning, then take a few minutes to visualize achieving a challenge you are currently facing. Using visualization can help you to change your emotional state to one of motivation.

So if you are struggling with a baby who wouldn't eat, then visualize yourself finally getting your baby to eat well and how incredibly happy that will make you feel. This will inspire you to take action and rekindle your motivation rather than feel stressed.

March 10
Positive Affirmation of the Day

Today is a day of positive affirmation. As you go through this day, repeat these words to yourself each time you find yourself drifting apart or feeling a little low.

"By being happy every day, I can help my children to become happy in their lives".

March 11
Show Gratitude

We spend so much time stressing over what we don't have that we forget to appreciate what we do have. When you are grateful for the things and people that you have in your life, then you will receive more. So make it a daily habit to record what you are grateful for. Write this down and then speak it out loud or think about it. This will give you that motivational boost to keep going.

March 12
Look at Both Sides of the Coin

Whenever an obstacle comes your way, it is important to remember this fact. If you only focus on the negatives (which most people do), it is much easier to get distraught, overwhelmed, and depressed by the situation. This will make it more challenging to overcome the obstacle.

However, if you look at the negatives and the positives, you see the obstacle in a much more realistic light. This realistic understanding of obstacles allows you to think rationally and clearly about the task at hand. From there, you can begin to overcome your obstacle instead of getting overwhelmed by it.

March 13
Enjoy those Moments Now

Can you remember how small your little one was when they were born? Can you see just how much they've changed over the last few days, weeks, months or years? This is just an indication of how fast they grow and how quickly they will soon move out of the house. So appreciate these precious moments right now whilst you can despite how exhausting it may seem. You will soon look back and actually miss these moments.

March 14
Watch Motivational Videos

One way to get your motivation back on track is to watch motivational videos on YouTube and other video sharing websites. Some of these motivational videos can be quite long so we recommend that you find a shorter video that will really inspire you. This will give you the motivational boost needed to get back on track.

March 15
Let it Go

Whenever we try to overcome obstacles that we can't beat, we get overwhelmed and blame ourselves. However do not get caught up on things that are beyond your control. Focusing on things outside of your control wastes your time and energy, and it may even hurt your self-esteem. Only focus on matters that you have some control in and if you cannot control the obstacle outcome in any way, let go of it.

March 16
Practice Makes Perfect

As the old saying goes, practice makes perfect. To beat any obstacle that comes your way, you have to practice overcoming them. By practicing, things will begin to get easier as you go. It takes practice to know how to balance raising kids with going back to work. It takes practice to set a bedtime routine for your children. So don't expect things to suddenly perfect themselves overnight; it will fall in place sooner than you know it.

March 17
Stay Optimistic

One of the best ways to ensure that you don't give up is to stay optimistic. For example if your baby refuses to eat solids but won't mind having their milk, then appreciate the fact that they at least aren't starving. Stay optimistic and look at the good in every obstacle.

March 18
Be Open to Change

Most people fear change but change is actually a good thing. Rather than going down the same path every day, you take a new one. If you've been using the same parenting strategy and it no longer seems to be working, you need to be willing to try something new.

Afterall your children are growing and changing every single day, meaning you will need to start implementing some new strategies to adapt to these new changes. So always be open minded to change - this will make things less stressful for you.

March 19
A Gentle Reminder

In case no one has told you this today, I just want you to remember that you are a great mother and doing absolutely amazing. So give yourself a pat in the back and go own it mama.

March 20
It's all Part of the Process

Facing some challenges? Don't be afraid of the challenges you face along the way. Not every obstacle has the potential to hurt you. It's all about perspective. Recognize the wall in front of you as an opportunity to grow. The person you become while going through your journey of motherhood, can be an unseen benefit you retain for the future.

March 21
Grow From It

To truly reach our greatness and our maximum potential as human beings, we must always be willing to grow, try new activities, and learn from the experiences we encounter - including the mistakes we make. The end goal however is to grow from it all.

March 22
Every Little Win Counts

Make sure to celebrate a little along the way mama! Don't forget to give yourself a pat on the back once in a while. Life is a process, and the little celebrations can save us from going insane. It's not a bad thing to enjoy yourself every so often. Do so in a positive way and continue to treat yourself as the glorious temple you are!

March 23
Mama You Did It

Today I want you to take a look at those little humans you created and appreciate how well you've raised them. That child(ren) didn't raise themselves, you were there every step of the way and sacrificed selflessly to ensure that they are here today, happy and healthy. You did it mama and you should absolutely be proud of yourself.

March 24
Positive Affirmation of the Day

Today is a day of positive affirmation. As you go through this day, repeat these words to yourself each time you find yourself drifting apart or feeling a little low.

"Being happy is a top priority in my life, and I remember to practice this feeling every day. I will allow myself to fully enjoy the little moments that I observe around me every day".

March 25
You are Everything and More

Hey mama, I know it can be hard to wake up every single day and have those little ones rely on you. But here's a reminder that you are everything and more to those little ones, and they are looking up to you. You are their comfort, their joy and their protector. So if there's anything you should know today, it's how special you are and what an amazing superhuman you are.

March 26
A Gentle Reminder

Today is just a gentle reminder for you to;

"look after yourself the same way you look after your little ones, and show yourself the same love you give your children".

~ Part 2 - Dealing with Loneliness & Isolation ~

One of the biggest struggles we encounter in our journey of motherhood is **loneliness**. And I don't mean loneliness from your kids but loneliness from friends, spouse and others around you. This is simply because we get so consumed raising those precious little ones that we barely even have time for ourselves - talkless of time for others.

Let's face it, as much as we might enjoy spending time with our little ones, there comes a time in life when you get tired of speaking in baby gibberish and some real adult interaction becomes essential. Plus if your kids are driving you crazy (which happens often) and you have no one to really talk to, this can be very detrimental to your emotional wellbeing.

So in the next few days we are going to be sharing some tips and strategies that should help minimize the issue of loneliness and get you back into the swing of things.

March 27
Find the Root Cause

The first step to dealing with loneliness is identifying what is really making you lonely. When you feel lonely, try to write out why you're feeling the way you are, the cause, the outcome, or anything else that comes to mind. Are you missing catching up with friends, family, or partners?

Do you miss the activities you used to do before you became a mother? And what could you do to fix this? Channelling your energy this way can help you become emotionally literate to mitigate the problem so you can transform yourself.

March 28
You Don't Have to Do it Alone

Just because we can figure things out by ourselves as mothers doesn't mean we have to. Sometimes we don't get the help we need because we simply do not ASK for it. And this can contribute greatly to us feeling very lonely.

Unfortunately when you don't ask for help, everyone assumes you have it all figured out. If you have a spouse, allow them to do the bedtime routine with the child, or even make dinner, do the laundry, clean the house or anything that can give you a little break.

Put your feet up, have a cup of tea, have a rest and allow yourself to be helped - without any guilt.

March 29
Be Open to Learning

Especially from other mothers that have been there. As much as we may try to do things alone, there is nothing more powerful than learning from someone who has been where you are and achieved the results you are aiming for.

When you open your mind up to learning from others who have been through what you are going through, you start to see things in a different light. So don't feel like you always have to figure things out alone or things must be done your way, instead be open to learning from more experienced people.

March 30
You Are Not Alone

Whatever you are going through, recognize that you are not alone in your struggle. We all face adversity.

Adversity rears its ugly head in many shapes and forms, yet is a common factor in all of our lives. It is good to remember that you are not the only person that experiences pain.

During the thick of the storm, it is easy to lose sight of the fact that most of the people you know are facing difficult trials of their own. By facing your challenges you are a step ahead in the game!

March 31
Join Groups & Forums

Most communities have local mum groups which you can join either in person or even virtually on platforms like Facebook Groups. This is a great place to connect with other mothers, learn from each other's experiences and actually mingle with other adults going through what you are experiencing right now.

Not only can this do wonders to your emotional well being, it can also eradicate those feelings of loneliness.

April

April 1
Hello April

Hey mama, welcome to another new month..
As you begin this new month, I want you to
step into it with a positive mindset. Because
the way you think can impact how you feel.
So today I want you to make this promise to
yourself.

*"I will focus on the good only and avoid any
negativity"*

Remember those words as you go through
this month and remind yourself of that each
time you are feeling a little low.

April 2
Get the Tunes On

The next time you feel yourself being lonely, tune in to your favourite music. Don't put those nursery rhymes or cartoons on. Crank up some music you love and dance to the beat. Your kids may look at you funny but don't be surprised to see them join in. What a great way to start the day, and do a little something fun with the kids. Plus it can do wonders to your mental health and state of mind.

April 3
Write Notes to Yourself

There is nothing more precious than receiving a written letter from a friend, loved one etc. What's even better is leaving yourself encouraging notes in places that you often look at, like your fridge, bedroom etc to make you feel better about yourself. Writing encouraging notes to yourself can remind you that you can overcome any challenge and feelings of loneliness.

April 4
Say Those Words Out Loud

One way to ensure that you stay happy is to say positive affirmations to yourself daily. When you repeatedly say something to yourself with deep conviction, you affirm in your mind and compel it to accept that suggestion and to work toward fulfilling it.

As soon as your mind accepts the suggestion as the absolute truth, it will focus its energy on it and make you take meaningful action to reach your goal.

So remember to speak those positive words out loud to yourself today - even if no one else does.

April 5
It's time for a Catch Up

Listening to nursery rhymes all day and dancing along with your kids may seem like fun. But when was the last time you called or met up with a friend? Not only is this great for your sanity but is a great way to give yourself a break from everything else. So call up that friend, and organise that catchup.

April 6
Speak it Out

As much as we try to keep it together as mothers, never be afraid to fully express your thoughts and feelings. Speak to a partner, friend, family or someone you trust if you find yourself struggling at any point. It's impossible for one human being to have everything figured out, so speaking out doesn't make you weak, it actually makes you a stronger person. Plus you will feel so much better and less lonely.

April 7
Dare to Do Something Different

When was the last time you did something fun? And I'm not referring to taking your kids to the park, or dancing to cocomelon in the living room. I mean something fun for YOU without the kids.

Like getting your hair done, going out for a drink with friends, having a getaway for yourself somewhere, or even treating yourself to something new? Well if you can't remember, then it means it's long overdue. So go book that spa, take that trip or even change your hair to a different colour.

April 8
Just Keep it Calm

Having one of those days? Take a step back today to calm down. A few minutes break would do you good. Wash your face, breath slowly and deeply, and notice if there is tension in any part of your body and release it. You can also listen to relaxing music, or call a friend or someone you trust. Releasing your inner feelings to a friend is a healthy option and can help minimize feelings of loneliness.

April 9
Have a Date Night

When was the last time you spent some alone time with your other half. Well now's time to plan for that date night. Go to that fancy restaurant you've been postponing for the longest time or go watch that movie. Leave the kids with their grandparents or someone who can help watch them for a few hours. If you don't have a partner, then plan a date night with your friends.

April 10
Trust Your Own Abilities

Most often we suffer from loneliness and isolation because we hate something in ourselves - not because we are really missing out on other people's company. Don't wait for people to tell you how much of an amazing mother you are.

Similarly, don't let other people's opinions or criticisms shake your confidence as a mother. Keep doing your best and most importantly give yourself some self love and appreciation for an amazing job. When you have a healthy attitude towards yourself, you will generally be content and feel less isolated.

April 11
Read A Book

You know how the saying goes "the more you learn the more you earn". Reading is a great way to not only improve your skills but can also be therapeutic in helping you overcome loneliness.

By focusing your energy on something positive like reading a book you love, you will realise that you are positively distracted, and this can equally keep your mind off any feelings of loneliness. So think about your hobbies and things you love and find some books around that niche to keep you busy and entertained.

April 12
Find A Hobby

When you have nothing but free time on your hands, it's easy to allow your mind to wander and stir up feelings of loneliness or negativity.

Looking after the kids isn't a hobby so you can cross that off your list. Honestly, there are so many interesting things to choose from. Chances are it won't be difficult to find something that you can be passionate about - something enjoyable you can turn to whenever you have time to spare. So dig deep into your hobbies and trust me you will find something.

April 13
Don't Isolate Yourself

Don't constantly subject yourself to a lonely environment. Even if you don't feel like talking to anyone or being around other people, force yourself to get out of the house instead of locking yourself up indoors. Sometimes the simple act of being around people is enough to combat loneliness. If you are feeling depressed and lonely, going for a walk or a drink can be enough to alleviate your loneliness.

April 14
Develop Your Mind

If you've always wanted to take up a new language or a subject that you've never been able to study before, now is a good time. Taking a college class, joining a book club or learning to cook a new cuisine can help you to connect with others.

Keeping your mind occupied will prevent you from constantly thinking about how alone you are, and by discussing subjects with others you will help them feel less lonely as well. Do not isolate yourself, loneliness can only be overcome if you make the effort to reach out and make that human connection with others.

April 15
Step Out of Your Comfort Zone

Connecting with the outside world and even nature can get you out of that funk of loneliness. So get out of the house. Take a walk in the sunshine with your little one. Go to the beach and enjoy the breeze. Go to church. Go to the mall and treat yourself to something nice. Go on a bus tour and just enjoy watching the world through the window. Look for a dance class in your local area. Or even join the gym.

You can even look for fun activities that you can do with your kids together. Once you start stepping outside your comfort zone and connecting with the real world, loneliness will become a thing of the past.

April 16
Stay Positive

Poor self-image and negative thoughts about yourself can make feelings of loneliness worse and keep you from seeking out contact with others.

Always try to avoid having self-deprecating thoughts by being as positive as you can be. By tackling this problem, you will feel more confident interacting with others and consequently help overcome the problem of loneliness.

April 17
Get Physical

If loneliness is sucking your energy levels, fight back by getting some exercise. Jogging or swimming can clear your head and boost your energy levels.

Group exercise programs at parks, community centers, etc. are also an excellent way to meet new people. Having an organized exercise program or exercise buddies gives you something to look forward to. Plus being physically fit helps relieve feelings of depression.

April 18
Spend Time with Someone Familiar

If it's companionship that you crave, pick up the phone and call up a family member or a friend that you haven't spoken to for a while. Everyone assumes that everyone else is too busy to hang out with them. But sometimes simply asking is the easiest thing that you can do to make or recreate that human connection

April 19
Listen to Inspiration

Had a lonely day or just felt like a hamster on a wheel? Then take a little time for yourself even if it's a few minutes after the child goes to sleep. Try not to distract yourself with anything else like housework, watching a movie or browsing on social media.

Put your headphones on, close your eyes and listen to some inspirational music or messages and watch how calm and relaxed you feel after that. You can also do this before you go to bed at night and see just how amazing you will feel when you wake up. This will also reassure you that you are not alone on this journey.

April 20
Get Comfortable Being Alone

Enjoy your own company. Take time out to get to know yourself better. Write a journal and chart your thoughts and feelings when you are feeling lonely. Take yourself out on dates, be it for dinner at a nice restaurant or a movie that you've been waiting to see. Once you are comfortable with your own company, other people are more likely to enjoy spending time with you as well.

April 21
Enrol for a Course

Take a course of study at your closest university or community college. Utilize it as a chance to learn about something you've forever wished to learn about. Get to connect with other students around you. You might discover somebody with other interests that you are able to spend time with when class is done. Plus this is a great way to take your mind off just being a mother.

April 22
Get Involved in a Local Cause

You won't have time to feel lonely if you are constantly helping others. It can be as simple as making an effort to listen to someone talk about their problems. If you have talent and skills in certain areas, you may also contribute your time to any number of charitable causes.

Checkout church groups,organizations, business clubs, local newspapers and many others for volunteer opportunities. Helping others will make you feel good about yourself, occupy your mind, and stop you from thinking about how alone you are. Having a shared interest is also a great way to develop new friendships.

April 23
Start That Business

Fortunately we live in a day and age where you can start a business right from the comfort of your home. And you don't need to have thousands in your bank account or take on a loan to get started. Thank God for social media and the internet. So think about your passions, hobbies, interests and things you are good at, and find ways to convert that into an online business.

Starting a business doing something you love isn't only going to bring in additional income, but you will have the opportunity to connect with clients, help people and get your mind off those feelings of loneliness.

(Visit www.startupreine.com for online business ideas you can start today)

~ Part 3 - Dealing with a Lack of Confidence & Self Esteem Issues ~

If there's anything in this world that will test your self confidence, it's being a mother. And even before you become a mother, the worries already start the moment they are in the womb.

Are they doing enough kicks? Are they comfortable? Am I feeding them properly? Am I capable of raising another human?

Then after they are born, you begin to doubt your own abilities.

Have the kids eaten well today? Am I feeding them the right nutrients? Are they getting enough sleep? Are they taking in enough breastmilk? Are they safe at daycare? Are they sleeping enough? Why aren't they on solids, crawling, walking, talking by the age the baby book says?

All of these thoughts can make you feel like you are doing the worst job at parenting, whilst constantly worrying about what you are doing right/wrong and doubting your own abilities.

So in the next few days we are going to be sharing some tips and strategies that should help minimize the issue of low self confidence and self esteem, and leave you feeling like the confident mother you were truly destined to be.

April 24
Change Your Mindset

Everything starts with your mindset and that includes boosting your self confidence. A shift in your mindset from negative to positive can have a dramatic impact on your confidence. Not only does a positive mindset trigger optimism, but it can help you achieve your goals better.

So instead of asking questions like "*Am I capable of being a good mother*" , replace that with "***I'm an amazing mother and doing a great job***".

Instead of saying "*Why isn't my child hitting developmental milestones at the time other kids are supposed to*", replace it with " ***My child is happy, healthy and will develop at their own pace because every child is different***".

Start cultivating a positive mindset and watch how your life and self confidence changes for the better.

April 25
Look at Past Achievements

This is a great self confidence boost. Your task here is to identify past achievements and successes in your life. For everything you achieved in the past you followed a number of steps. You used a process that was right for you to accomplish whatever it was that you set out to do.

So when you are feeling like you can't handle things today, look back at all those difficult tasks you thought you couldn't handle like pushing out that baby, and bringing an actual human being to the world. Relive your past accomplishments with passion and realize that you can achieve whatever obstacle is coming your way.

April 26
Positive Affirmation of the Day

Today is a day of positive affirmation. As you go through this day, repeat these words to yourself each time you find yourself drifting apart or feeling a little low.

"My mind is completely free of resistance and is open to all the new and exciting possibilities before me".

April 27
Put on Some Makeup

Or anything that makes you feel beautiful. You are naturally beautiful already. However there's just something powerful about enhancing your beauty. By just wearing some makeup, stirring at yourself in the mirror and appreciating how beautiful you look. This might just be the little boost of self confidence you need today to make yourself feel better. So go wear some makeup today and remind yourself how stunning you are.

April 28
Visualize Yourself Succeeding

When you start going through the process of raising children, you will realise that your confidence is tested a few times. You will have to find ways to work on your self-confidence.

One great way to build your self confidence is to visualize yourself succeeding in that difficult situation for at least five minutes every day and then tackling it the best way you can. The more confident you become, the less stressful it will be for you.

April 29
Take a Look in the Mirror

There may be some days when you look in the mirror and don't like what you see. Especially for us mothers going through all the incredible changes with our bodies.

Sometimes it may even seem like we just "let go". This can quickly kill any motivation you have and quickly ruin your day. So today I want you to look at yourself in the mirror, and think of 3 things you are grateful for, even if you don't feel like it. Repeat it to yourself 3 times and this will help you get through your day on a more positive note.

April 30
Avoid Limiting Beliefs

When you are constricted by your limiting beliefs and a lack of confidence, you will do far fewer things over the course of your life. For example, if you believe that you are not a good mother, you will probably never experience the beauty that motherhood has to offer and will constantly feel stressed out about the process.

Don't let negative beliefs crowd your mind, rather tell yourself you can do it and take it one day at a time.

May

May 1
Happy New Month

Hey mama, welcome to another new month. As you begin this new month, I want you to step into it with a positive mindset. Because the way you think can impact how you feel. So today I want you to make this promise to yourself.

"I will be kind to myself this month"

Remember those words as you go through this month and affirm them to yourself each time you are feeling a little low.

May 2
Make Yourself Presentable

Take the time to make yourself look presentable today. Make sure that you wear something cute (not those joggers or pyjamas) and that you are properly groomed.

Do your hair, shave your legs, exfoliate. Once you have cleaned yourself up, look at yourself in the mirror and think of the three favorite things about your appearance that you like. This positive thinking will help to build your confidence and serve as a reminder of how beautiful you are each time you feel a little low.

May 3
Get Journaling

The only way you can begin to overcome your limiting beliefs is to identify them. One way you can determine those beliefs that are holding you back is by journaling. You need to find time every day to sit down and write about your current situation. Then you need to understand what is causing you to feel that way. Journaling will help you discover your limiting beliefs, which is one of the first steps to overcoming them.

May 4
Talk to Yourself

It sounds crazy but it works. All of us have a running monologue constantly in our heads, whether we realize it or not. Everything we see, hear, or touch sparks off an immediate dialog in our thoughts.

Negative thoughts literally suck energy from our minds and bodies and block the flow of positive messages. You need to hear the positive messages as they will build your self confidence and raise your self esteem. Take control. Use your inner thoughts to talk to yourself in a positive manner, as often as you can.

May 5
Boost Your Skills

You are your biggest asset. And investing in yourself is one of the best things you could ever do to boost your self esteem. Knowledge is power and consistently boosting your skills through taking an online course or even reading a book can open doors to great opportunities you could never have imagined. So never ever stop investing in yourself and learning - even as a mother.

May 6
Mind Your Words

The words you use have a lot more power than you think. How you talk about your life is how your life will be. Your mind hears what you say about yourself and your life. If you describe your life as boring, hectic, chaotic, that's exactly how it will be.

However, if you view your life in a positive light, you will see your life in an entirely different way which can boost your self esteem.

May 7
Mind Your Company

The people that you spend time around can have a considerable influence on your self-esteem. Your friends can help build your self-confidence, your self-image, and self-respect, or they can bring it down. Unfortunately, there are those in our lives that will purposely try to harm our self-esteem to build themselves up.

Ever been in that situation where someone is telling you how to raise your kids, and making you feel like your parenting style is vile? Yes, try to avoid those people because that can have a blow on your self esteem and confidence as a mother.

Now there's a difference between someone advising you because they genuinely care, and plainly criticizing you to feel better about themselves. Learn to spot the difference and excuse yourself if it feels uncomfortable.

May 8
Positive Affirmation of the Day

Today is a day of positive affirmation. As you go through this day, repeat these words to yourself each time you find yourself drifting apart or feeling a little low.

"I have the potential, power, and ability to create all the success, prosperity and abundance that I desire in my life".

May 9
Delete that Social Media App

Hello to the generation of perfectly curated pictures of perfect lives on Instagram. From the mother who has snapped back to a size 0 after her 3rd kid, to the mother whose kids always seem put together, well behaved and appear faultless. Meanwhile your house is looking a mess, kids are drawing on the wall, and the last time you had a shower was a week ago.

It's no wonder we find ourselves comparing our real lives to someone else's fake life on social media. Our complete obsession with social media, contributes to the widespread self-esteem issues that we face. Remember people only share the joys but hardly ever the pains. So if you find that you are constantly comparing yourself to that perfect instagram mama, celebrity etc and it's starting to impact your self confidence, unfollow them or take a break from the app altogether and delete it from your phone.

May 10
Learn to Accept Compliments

When we feel bad about ourselves, it can be hard for anyone else to drag us out. During these times, we tend to be more resistant to compliments. Rather than shrugging off compliments as lies, you should try to set the goal of tolerating compliments when you receive them. This is important to do, even if it feels uncomfortable because it will help boost your self esteem.

May 11
Remind Yourself of Your Worth

Reminding yourself of your real worth is the best way to revive low self-esteem when your confidence sustains a blow. When you feel this way, write down everything that makes you a valuable mother and all the amazing things you've accomplished so far as a mother - even when you thought you couldn't.

Remind yourself of this each time you feel a blow on your self confidence and recognise yourself for it.

May 12
Stop Criticizing Yourself

We are more likely to kick ourselves when we are down. When we have low self-esteem, we tend to do even more damage to it by being self-critical.

When you start to tell yourself all the things that you are doing wrong and criticizing yourself for who you are, think twice about what you are saying. By taking a few minutes to recognize the self-criticism, you will give yourself the ability to start building yourself up instead.

May 13
Toss it in the Bin

If you have negative thoughts, write them down on a scrap of paper, screw the paper up into a ball and throw it into the trash can. By doing this you are telling yourself these thoughts are nothing but rubbish and that's where they belong. Watch how great you feel after you do that.

May 14
Always Stay Prepared

The more prepared you are for any given situation, the more confident you'll feel about your competency and expertise. Be prepared that your kid may wake up in the middle of the night, they may fall ill anytime, you may get a call from daycare whilst at work, they may soil themselves whilsts out and about, they may refuse to eat that meal it took you 10 hours to prepare, etc.

However, being prepared shouldn't be confused with worrying all the time to the point it consumes your life, it just means you shouldnt expect things to always go as planned especially with kids. Being prepared will help you to avoid getting tripped up by life's unexpected challenges.

May 15
Meditation is key

One great way to boost your self esteem is to practice meditation. Find somewhere quiet where you are able to relax for 5 or 10 minutes, close your eyes and let your mind empty of all thoughts and feelings. Begin to repeat your affirmation to yourself over and over again while concentrating on the words you are repeating and believe in what you are saying.

May 16
Say a Prayer

Praying is another great way to have some peace and quiet and take your mind off all the overwhelm. Just a few words of prayer first thing in the morning can have a huge impact on how you feel during the rest of the day.

When you talk to God (or whatever power you believe in) you feel a sense of peace and tranquility within you - this is called faith. It's like God's way of reassuring you that he's got you and there's a greater power watching over you which can make you feel safe, at peace and more confident.

May 17
Self Affirmation

The trick to making lasting changes is to shift the way you view yourself. We tend to believe what we tell ourselves, so repeating positive affirmations daily will help to boost your self-confidence.

To get your mind to accept the positive affirmations quickly, phrase them as a question. So instead of saying;

"today I will be kind to myself"

You could replace that with

"Am I being kind to myself today?"

Our brains are wired to seek answers to a question, and by asking questions, you can quickly analyze things and examine yourself.

May 18
Become Your Own Mentor

Another technique you can use to overcome self esteem is to become your own mentor. Pretend that you are sitting across from your future self. Not only are they kind and wise, but they've achieved everything that you wanted in your life.

Have a conversation with your future self and tell them about the areas in your life where you're currently having trouble. Ask them to help you uncover your limiting beliefs, discover how you formed your limiting beliefs, how to interpret the situation differently, and help you come up with a new set of beliefs.

This will also help you visualize better where you plan to be and what goals you aim to achieve in the future.

May 19
Do Something that Scares You

The best way for you to overcome fear is to face it head-on. Getting out of your comfort zone and facing your fears will help you to gain more confidence. By doing something that scares you instead of telling yourself you can't do it, you'll start to gain confidence from those experiences and will quickly notice a boost in your self-confidence.

May 20
Positive Affirmation of the Day

Today is a day of positive affirmation. As you go through this day, repeat these words to yourself each time you find yourself drifting apart or feeling a little low.

"Today I wake up with a happy smile on my face and tremendous gratitude in my heart for all the wonderful moments that await me during the day".

May 21
Reward Without Guilt

Being a mother is hectic as it is - from juggling those challenging activities to feeling like a walking garbage. And the worst part is, you don't really get a pat in the back or reward most times for all that hard work which can usually have a blow on your confidence.

So don't forget to reward yourself for all your hard work - even if it means indulging yourself in some of those guilty pleasures like ice cream, cookies, a glass of wine, or splurging on a nice gift for yourself. And do not ever feel guilty for rewarding yourself because you deserve the world mama.

May 22
Stay Committed

You should take positive action and decide exactly what it is you wish to achieve in life. Once you have set your mind on what you want, you should go into it with utter conviction and commitment.

When you are planning and setting out your goal you have to have firm conviction that you will achieve your goal whatever it takes, you should visualize your goal from beginning to end and see yourself achieving whatever it is you set out to do. Doing so will greatly boost your self esteem and confidence.

May 23
Get Visualizing

Visualization is a powerful technique that requires you to see a picture of yourself that you are proud of, in your mind. When struggling with low self-esteem, we often have a poor perception of ourselves that tends to be inaccurate. Practice visualizing a beautiful version of yourself being an amazing mother and achieving your goals. This will help you boost your confidence.

May 24
Shift to Positive

A great way to boost your confidence is to shift your mindset from negative to positive. This can have a dramatic impact on your life and self esteem. Not only does a positive mindset trigger optimism, but it can help keep you focused towards achieving anything you set your mind to. Start cultivating a positive mindset and watch how your life changes for the better.

May 25
Be Confident in Yourself

The more confident you are as a mother, the less stressful things can be for you. To gain more confidence in your own abilities and instincts, first, look back upon the successes you've had in your life.

This can be from pushing out that baby, giving them their first bath, figuring out how to breastfeed, balancing work and motherhood, etc. Look back at any and all of these successes and realize that you have the ability to achieve great successes and accomplishments. And you have already achieved several, even if you don't think about them often.

This can increase your confidence that you have what it takes to succeed in this world and need to trust those skills and instincts more.

May 26
Do Whatever it Takes

Thinking and visualisation can help boost your self esteem. But only to a certain extent. You need to be willing to take action and the steps required to get to where you want to be.

For example, instead of trying to do everything at once which could overwhelm you and have a blow on your confidence as a mother, why not enjoy some undistracted time with your little one, give them full attention and actually enjoy the moment.

Remember these precious moments won't last long. By taking action, you are actually addressing the problem at hand and tackling any obstacles hindering your self esteem and confidence.

May 27
Your Mental Health Matters

In order to live a happier, healthier life you should take care of not only your physical health but also your mental health.

There are so many different ways to look after your mental health such as; learning to manage your day and time better, focusing on completing one task at a time before moving on to another, being flexible in your thinking, taking small breaks throughout the day, trying not to do everything, and never over exerting your body.

Try to figure out whatever is affecting your mental health and find ways to work on it. This would consequently have a positive impact on your self esteem.

May 28
Surround Yourself with Positivity

When you start to feel tired or ready to give up, look at the people you have chosen to surround yourself with. It is essential to make sure that you are getting as much, if not more than you are giving out. To help you stay motivated, you need to surround yourself with positive people.

May 29
Question Your Inner Critic

Some of the harshest comments that we hear come from ourselves, via our inner critic. When your inner critic becomes overactive and inaccurate, you may start to suffer from low self-esteem. To help combat your inner critic, look for evidence to support or deny the things that it is saying to you. Find opportunities to compliment, congratulate, and reward yourself, even for your smallest accomplishments.

May 30
Think Like a Child

Yes for a change! Children are so carefree, honest and fun. Think about what you used to do for fun as a child. When you ask kids what they want to be when they grow up, they bring up all sorts of ideas of what they aspire to become.

When you switch from that mindset of being an adult to thinking like a kid, you start to realise anything is possible if you set your mind to it. Ok maybe not that part of wanting to grow up to become a dinosaur. But I'm sure you get the idea.

Don't overthink things, try to do something fun and tell yourself you are going to be the best mother you can possibly be. And have fun!

May 31
The Sky is Your Limit

You can accomplish anything you set your mind to - the sky really is your limit. The key is to stay committed to achieving what it is you want, set your mind to taking whatever steps are needed to accomplish what you want, and change your approach until you've gotten the results you want. Don't give up, keep going because you are doing an amazing job as a mother.

~ Part 4 - Beauty & Skin Care Tips for Mothers ~

Skin Care is probably one of the most neglected areas of our lives as mothers. Usually because we spend so much time caring for our children, the house, the husband that we somewhat forget to care for ourselves. For some mothers it is perceived and viewed as an occasional pamper treat when it should really be a part of your day to day routine. Skincare is an extremely important way to look after ourselves and avoid ageing prematurely.

By incorporating natural skincare habits into your daily routine, you'll both feel and look your very best. So in the next few days we are going to be talking about natural skincare remedies to keep you looking and feeling beautiful.

<u>Important Note:</u> It's important that you seek the advice and approval from your healthcare provider or a dermatologist prior to making any drastic changes to your skin, diet or exercise.

June

June 1
Happy New Month

Hey mama, welcome to another new month..
As you begin this new month, I want you to
step into it with a positive mindset. Because
the way you think can impact how you feel.
So today I want you to make this promise to
yourself.

"I will focus on the good only and avoid any
negativity"

Remember those words as you go through
this month and remind yourself of that each
time you are feeling a little low.

June 2
Glow with Meditation

One great skin care tip is meditation. When we relax and calm our minds, focusing only on our breathing, we tend to look at everything around us in a brand new light. Having a more positive outlook means less stress on our bodies, which equates to an overall natural and healthy glow.

June 3
Rejuvenate Your Eyes

Our eyes love to show our current physical and mental state. As mothers, this is the first thing that people around you will notice when you're exhausted. There are plenty of eye treatments on the market that promise to do all of this, but buyer beware.

Steer clear of those with too many chemicals, and look for ones that are primarily made up of caffeine and B vitamins.

Thanks to the power of caffeine though, you don't have to look too far for a natural way to de-puff your peepers! Better yet, try this easy at-home remedy.

All you need to do is steep two, caffeinated tea bags in very hot water for about a minute or so. Then place both of them on a plate and put them in your refrigerator to chill.

Once they're nice and cold, put one on each of your closed eyelids for up to 15 minutes. Voila! Goodbye tired eyes and hello, sunshine! To really see the difference, consider taking a before and after shot of your eyes.

June 4
Lime for Skincare

If you have any dark spots on your skin that you'd like to brighten, then invest in some limes and cotton balls. Simply take a bit of lime juice, dip a cotton ball in it, and apply it to the affected area for about a half an hour. And if you suffer from loose skin, then good news: it helps with that too!

In addition to all the above, lime juice is also full of antibiotic properties that help inhibit the growth of acne-causing bacteria. The natural bleaching properties will help give your skin an overall glow. You can even consider using lime peel as a scrub, too.

June 5
Positive Affirmation of the Day

Today is a day of positive affirmation. As you go through this day, repeat these words to yourself each time you find yourself drifting apart or feeling a little low.

"I am ready to tackle whatever comes my way with happiness and a positive attitude".

June 6
Tea Tree Oil

You've probably heard about the many benefits of tea tree oil, which is derived from Melaleuca Alternifolia, also known as Tea Trees. Tea Tree oil is great for soothing dry skin, and its natural antiseptic qualities help combat oily skin as well. So, if you have either dry or oily skin, look for a natural lotion that contains real tea tree oil. It's important that it be diluted, since Tea Tree oil is so potent.

June 7
Don't forget your Beauty Sleep

When you go to bed after a long day, your main goal is to recharge your internal clock. But what you might not know, is that as that's happening, your skin is naturally rejuvenating itself. So not only do you need a good night's sleep to physically function, but your skin needs it too!

To ensure that you rest long enough every night, make sure to maintain a peaceful and relaxing bedroom atmosphere. Turn off all mobile devices and invest in a good mattress. Also try reading before you go to bed instead of watching television.

June 8
Hydration is Key

We hear it all the time: drinking water is so important, and for good reason. Our body is made up of more than 50% water, which we lose throughout the day when we perspire. But it's not just our internal body that takes a hit when we become dehydrated.It shows in our face, too.

Drinking plenty of water not only helps get rid of that bloat, flushes out toxins within our body but can also help with conditions like adult acne. Some of the toxins that contribute to adult acne can easily be flushed away with higher water intake.

As you can see, you don't need to invest in expensive skincare just try sneaking in a little more water, then watch and feel your skin get back to its glory days!

June 9
Face Steaming for Beauty

Steaming your face opens your pores, which means it loosens all of that built-up gunk and dirt. It also gets rid of acne-causing bacteria as well. It opens your pores, which is great if you suffer from millia: small, white bumps on your face that are full of oil.

Also it enhances circulation, which is perfect for maintaining a youthful glow. To do an at-home steaming session, simply boil some water, place in a heatproof bowl, drape a towel over your neck, and steam for 10-15 minutes before patting dry.

June 10
The Power of Coconut Oil

Want to minimize the risk of getting a skin infection? Then coconut oil is the answer. Not only is coconut oil good for your physical health, but it also has many benefits when applied directly to your skin.

By incorporating coconut oil into your natural skincare routine, your chances of developing a skin infection drastically diminishes. You can easily incorporate coconut oil into your natural skincare by using it as a body moisturizer, hair mask, and even as a facial moisturizer.

Start by using it on a small patch of your skin and see how you react. If you're unsure of your skin type, then consult with a physician who can make that determination with you.

June 11
Take a Deep Shower

I'm not referring to a quick 5 minute dash in the bathroom because you are in a hurry to drop your little ones off to school or head to work.

I'm talking about a proper long shower where you can spend 15-20 minutes giving your body the tender, love and care it deserves.

Taking a nice long shower isn't only a great way to keep your body clean, it can be extremely therapeutic and leave you feeling relaxed. So don't forget to give yourself a nice long shower or better still a bath today.

June 12
The Power of Shea Butter

Shea butter is popping up everywhere nowadays. The next time you're at the store, take a look at the skincare aisle and notice how many lotions contain this natural moisturizer. It's popular for many reasons, one of them being that it encourages natural collagen production.

Collagen is what our skin needs to feel full and lustrous, filling out those fine lines and wrinkles. And it's perfect for all skin types, which means you can reap the benefits whether your skin is dry, combination, or oily!

Shea butter also melts at body temperature, which makes it perfect for absorbing it through our pores. Like some other items mentioned on here, it's also high in fatty acids that our skin needs.

It's also anti-aging, which is a big plus when it comes to natural skincare. When used regularly, it can also help to prevent stretch marks! There are plenty of natural shea butter lotions that you can buy, but you can also purchase pure shea butter and apply it directly to your skin.

~ Part 5 - Dealing with Tiredness & Fatigue ~

Tiredness and exhaustion are common issues we mothers face. It feels almost as if life has been drained outside of us. Of course a big contributing factor to this is motherhood and all the activities that come with raising children.

Whilst we may not be able to control the tiredness that comes with raising children, there are certain changes and things that can be done to make the experience less stressful and consequently leave you feeling energized.

So in the next few days we are going to look at different ways to combat and overcome fatigue so that you can get your life back.

June 13
Track Your Time

If you don't know how much you're really doing, it can be easy to just keep going 24/7 and never take a break. Take some time to track what you're doing daily for about a week.

Pay attention to those times that you are not busy with the kids, what other things do you spend your time doing? You can use your smartphone to track your activities or you can go old school and carry around a small notebook to record your activities in.

This will help you track all those unnecessary activities sucking up your time and making you exhausted so you can begin to eliminate them.

June 14
Get a Good Night's Sleep

Don't forget how important sleep is. Most adults should seek to get between six and eight hours a night. It can also largely depend on your genetics how much sleep feels right for you. Work with what you know you need.

If you're having trouble sleeping at night, address that issue so that you fall asleep fast and your sleeping time is productive. To help get used to this process, go to bed and wake up at the same time every day for at least 30 days.

You can start with the least time and work your way up to find out which amount of time works best for you to make you feel rested each day.

June 15
It's Ok to Do Nothing

A lot of mothers tend to be uncomfortable with downtime. They feel as if they're slackers. But, even if you have a mentally exhausting job as compared to a physically exhausting one, everyone needs some downtime. So remember that you need some downtime to do absolutely nothing.

June 16
Avoid Dehydration

It can be very easy to get dehydrated. Even mild dehydration will slow down circulation in your body. Most adults should drink between 8-ounce glasses of water each day to stay hydrated. If you exercise strenuously you'll need more. Tea, coffee, soda, and sugary drinks (even fake sugar) are all dehydrating and don't do the same thing as clean, filtered water will. Take the challenge and commit to drinking enough water for 30 days, and you'll see a huge difference.

June 17
Monitor Your Activities

Look at the things in your life that are draining your energy and remove them. Rather than being an additive way to improve your energy, this is a subtractive method. In other words, you are improving your energy by doing less and not more, which is considerably easier when your energy is low to begin with. Plus taking on too much can be exhausting.

June 18
Minimize Caffeine Intake

If you use caffeine to power you through the day, then this is something you should look at stopping right away. Caffeine can actually severely hamper your energy levels and may even be what makes it so hard to get up in the morning. It may seem to give you a temporal artificial feeling of energy and drive but this eventually leads to withdrawal leaving you tired and groggy all the time.

June 19
Procrastination is a Drainer

Procrastinating wastes your valuable time without giving you the permission you need to properly rest. Worst of all is procrastinating late at night and watching tv, browsing on social media for instance into the early hours of the morning because you can't be bothered to get ready for bed. Not only would this leave you feeling more tired in the morning, but can also leave you feeling exhausted. So try to stay away from those distractions especially when it's time to go to sleep.

June 20
Splash Some Cold Water

Splashing some cold water on your face can instantly give you an energy boost for a number of reasons.

One benefit of doing this is that it encourages blood flow to your face and thus your brain, giving you a little more fuel for thinking and staying awake.

Moreover, the body reacts to cold by producing more norepinephrine. This is a stimulating neurotransmitter which helps us become more focused and more awake!

June 21
Boost it Up

A quick workout is fantastic for boosting energy levels. This doesn't have to mean going to the gym and lifting weights either. Simply doing a few press-ups can help to get your blood flowing, produce endorphins and clear away brain fog.

In fact, if you can't muster a few press ups, even just jumping up and down lightly on the spot is a great way to boost your energy levels and avoid exhaustion.

June 22
Do Something You Love

Sometimes the worst thing you can do for your energy levels is to power through when you're feeling tired and lethargic. Instead, try doing something that you really enjoy for 10 minutes, whether that is blasting the tunes or reading a chapter of a great book. This will re-engage you and bring back some enthusiasm which is excellent for energy.

June 23
Feel the Sun

Go and stand outside for a moment and feel the sun on your face. This is highly invigorating and will help to remind your body clock that it's still day time, while at the same time triggering the production of vitamin D and other important hormones that can help with fatigue.

June 24
Alcohol is a Killer

Here comes the bad news: alcohol is very bad for your energy levels and can leave you completely exhausted. This is because alcohol is actually a depressant. Alcohol works in the *opposite* manner to a stimulant. And because it causes whole brain areas to stop working, it can rob you of your higher order brain function too. A little occasional glass of wine wont hurt after a stressful day but don't make it an everyday habit.

June 25
Avoid Sitting Too Much

With mothers constantly on their feet running errands and cleaning up after the kids, sitting too much is probably far from a problem you will face. However if you are someone that sits a lot, or likes to spend your evenings relaxing in front of the television: you almost certainly sit too much as well.

Thus, if you are spending a lot of time just sitting down, this can have an impact on your energy levels. Try to walk around and incorporate some movement in between sitting. Take a ten minute break every hour or so and if you need to take a call, try pacing around the office while you take it.

June 26
Try Some Almonds

Almonds contain magnesium and B vitamins that help to convert food into energy. When you have low magnesium levels, you become tired more quickly, while insufficient levels of B vitamins can lead to a decrease in concentration, irritability, and fatigue. To get an instant boost in energy, eat one ounce of almonds and feel the energy recharge.

June 27
Don't Ignore Power Naps

Pushing yourself too hard can quickly zap energy, which is almost unavoidable to us mothers. However, taking a 60-minute power nap is essential and can do wonders to your energy levels.

The secret is to aim to nap for around 60 minutes. You don't want to sleep too long or sleep very little.

In this time you will go through one complete sleep cycle and will go from the lightest stage of sleep, to SWS (slow wave sleep) to REM. You'll then be woken up just as you start to come around. This is also instrumental in helping us lay down new memories and boost our performance and energy levels.

June 28
Grab a Banana

Bananas are filled with potassium, fiber, and vitamin B6, nutrients that promote muscle function and sustained energy. They are especially significant as a pre or post-workout snack.

Create an even more energizing combo by pairing a banana with a cup of yogurt or a glass of low-fat milk. Consider eating a banana in the morning to fuel your body for the better part of the morning and feel the boost in your energy levels.

June 29
Start the Day Right

Too many of us wake up feeling groggy, lethargic and tired and as a result we waste the first half of the day. Some of us will even feel very sick in the morning, or have bad headaches.

This can be linked to a number of factors such as stress, dehydration, low blood sugar, or other underlying health conditions. This can consequently have a negative impact on your energy levels during the rest of the day.

A few things that could help is having a healthy breakfast, taking a shower in the morning, meditation and starting the day with a positive mindset.

June 30
Breathing is Essential

Breathing is one of your most critical bodily functions. The simple act of breathing can have a substantial impact on both your emotional and physiological states.

Conscious breathing exercises can help to rebalance your mind and body and boost your energy levels.

Take a deep breath, slowly inhaling through your nose, count to six, and hold your breath, then exhale through your mouth for a count of six. Repeat this seven times throughout the day.

July

July 1
Happy New Month

Hey mama, welcome to another new month..
As you begin this new month, I want you to
step into it with a positive mindset. Today I
want you to make this promise to yourself.

*"I will not let anything get in the way of
being the best mother I can be"*

Remember those words as you go through
this month and remind yourself of that each
time you are feeling a little low.

July 2
Avoid too Much Time Inside

Being cooped up inside all day, without sunlight and fresh air, you will likely find yourself fatigued. Often the air indoors is stuffy and infused with toxins like chemicals from synthetic materials and air fresheners.

Artificial lighting can also deplete your energy and may cause you to have trouble falling asleep, and wake up still drained.

So try going out for a short walk and take a breathe of fresh air with the kids, not only is this great for your mental health but can do wonders to your energy levels. Plus the kids will sleep better at night.

July 3
Watch Out Blood Sugar Levels

One thing we often neglect as mothers is our diets. We either forget to eat completely, or just grab the quickest thing to eat which most often may not be the healthiest. Foods that are loaded with simple carbs and sugar will increase your blood sugar.

Constant blood sugar spikes followed by sharp crashes will cause you to feel fatigued over the course of your day. Try eating lean protein and whole grains at every meal to keep your blood sugar levels stable.

July 4
Limit Screen Time

According to a recent study conducted by Dr. Marc Bergman, a neuroscientist at the University of Michigan, television isn't as restful as you may think.

As we age, smartphones and TVs have fewer and fewer stress-reducing benefits. Rather than turning to a screen to unwind, it is recommended that you read, talk with friends, work out, or go for a walk.

Disconnecting from technology can help to clear your mind before bed, resulting in improved quality of sleep and increased energy.

July 5
Practice Some Yoga

While most exercise is good for increasing energy levels, yoga may be especially beneficial when you need to increase your energy.

Practicing yoga once a week for just six weeks has been shown to improve your mind's clarity, energy, and confidence. Practicing yoga will not only help increase your energy, but it is also excellent for regaining your balance. Plus it can also help you deal with exhaustion and fatigue.

July 6
Know Your Body Clock

You may get your burst of energy first thing in the morning, or you may do your best at the end of the day.

Everyone has differences in their daily energy patterns, which are determined by your brain structure and genetics.

This can be challenging to change. So it's best to learn your body, then schedule demanding activities when your energy levels are at their peak.

July 7
Increase Magnesium Intake

Having low levels of magnesium can result in easily feeling out of breath and having an increased heart rate. This is an indication that your body is working harder, which can quickly drain your energy and make you feel exhausted.

It is vital that you get the recommended amount of magnesium in your diet if you want to eliminate fatigue. Some excellent sources of magnesium include fish, like halibut, whole grains, almonds, hazelnuts, and cashews. There are also supplements you could take to increase these levels if you simply don't have the time or are unable to consume these foods.

July 8
Time Your Eating

Properly timing your meals can have a profound effect on your metabolism and energy. Eating too much or too little can make you feel lethargic and can disrupt blood sugar levels, resulting in chronic fatigue. Timing your meals will ensure that you will have enough energy to get through the day and accomplish your tasks without feeling exhausted afterward.

July 9
Do Absolutely Nothing

We spend all the time running after the kids, cooking, cleaning and everything else that comes with being a mother. So pick a day, take some time off, drop the kids with the grandparents, your partner and spend the day doing absolutely nothing. Because you deserve a day to yourself of doing absolutely nothing.

July 10
Check Your Iron Levels

If you have an iron deficiency, you could begin to feel sluggish, irritable, weak, and unable to focus. With an iron deficiency, less oxygen is able to travel to your muscles and cells, leaving you feeling more tired. Reduce your risk of anemia by boosting your iron intake via eating more lean beef, eggs, kidney beans, nuts, dark green leafy vegetables and peanut butter.

July 11
Shed Some Weight

Losing the extra weight can provide you with a powerful boost of energy. Even small reductions in your body fat can help to improve your mood and quality of life. Try cutting back on portion sizes, eating balanced meals, and increasing your physical activity to get rid of the extra weight that is depleting your energy.

July 12
Just Dance

Dancing is one of the most enjoyable forms of exercise and can help you combat stress while toning your muscles. Dancing is also one of the most effective ways to manage your weight.

So blast up some of your favourite tunes and even get the kids involved. This can leave you feeling happy and boost your energy levels, which can be extremely beneficial when you are fighting fatigue.

July 13
Engage in a Relaxing Hobby

Hobbies that promote relaxation are great for when you need to unwind after a long day at work or an afternoon of strenuous activity. Rather than reaching for the TV remote or video game controller when you need to relax, you need to find a relaxing activity like gardening, reading or even dancing.

Unfortunately, TV and video games require your mind to continue to work, which can increase your stress, even if you are just sitting on the couch. Engaging in relaxing activities will relax both your mind and body because they don't require you to overthink and are not physically strenuous.

July 14
Do Not Oversleep

Having too much of anything is bad for you. So when you decide to let out your inner lethargic lion sleep for over 10 hours a day, you'll start feeling different side effects. Instead of a light fuzzy head, you'll have a heavy throbbing head, pulsating because it's been out of work for once again, far too long. This can leave you feeling even more tired than you were before.

July 15
Eat Smaller Snacks

Overeating at meal time isn't good because it can make you feel bloated, heavy, which can result in feeling too lazy and tired to move. It is far better for you and your energy level to eat small meals with snacks in between, rather than eating less frequently, but overeating at every meal.

This is what is known as power snacking. By eating small snacks between meals, you keep your blood sugar up and your energy levels high. You can snack on yogurt, fruits, cheese, and nuts to keep you from getting too hungry between meals.

July 16
Practice Meditation

Meditation is a powerful tool that you can use to help you manage stress, eliminate fatigue, and improve the overall quality of your life. It has also been shown to improve your cognitive function and increase your energy and vitality when practiced regularly. When you meditate regularly, you are training your body to relax.

July 17
Learn to Rest

When you rest, you lower the levels of cortisol that your body is producing. Cortisol is released when you become stressed and high levels of cortisol in your blood are associated with fatigue, increased blood pressure, and weight gain. So learn to have some rest when needed.

July 18
Listen to Relaxing Music

Recent studies have shown that listening to soothing music can reduce stress, anxiety, and fatigue. It has also been shown to help you get a good night's sleep, reduce insomnia, which can help you further fight fatigue. Music helps to calm us down, relax our muscles, reduce stress, decrease blood pressure, and improve the heart rate. So try listening to soothing music, in the mornings and before you go to bed at night.

July 19
Delegate Tasks

Another great way to stop yourself from becoming fatigued is to delegate tasks. This can be anything from hiring a nanny, babysitter or even getting family to watch the kids for a few hours a day saving you from over exerting yourself. Understanding that you don't have to do everything yourself can be extremely beneficial in reducing exhaustion and enhancing your energy.

July 20
Learn to Say "No"

To prevent fatigue as a mother, you need to learn what your limitations are both physically and mentally. It is important that you learn how to say "**NO**" if you don't think that you can take on any more tasks or responsibilities. You should always put yourself first and not try to take on more than you can actually handle.

July 21
Don't be Hard on Yourself

Most of the stress that we experience in our lives is self-induced. If you want to combat stress and eliminate fatigue from your life, then you have to avoid being too hard on yourself. Avoid burning the candle at both ends. Take the time to relax and recharge yourself and avoid working too hard and pushing yourself to the point of extreme exhaustion.

July 22
Create Healthy Boundaries

You may feel like you want to please everyone around you. However, trying to please everyone, all the time can become incredibly frustrating and lead to increased levels of stress and fatigue. To increase your energy, you will need to create healthy personal boundaries.

~ Part 6 - How to Manage Time & Stay Organized ~

Oh the precious T word we mothers never seem to have. From keeping late nights breastfeeding to cleaning after the kids 24/7, it becomes almost impossible to find the time to do anything.

Time management is necessary for almost anyone in this super busy world we live in. However, this is even harder for mothers because we are responsible for keeping our families together. Our days are filled with running around for our children, working on multiple projects and trying to juggle everything.

If you are finding that you are pressed for time or trying to juggle everything, then in the next few days, we are going to be exploring some tips to help you manage your time better as you go through this journey of motherhood.

July 23
Wake Up a Little Earlier

Once you've established a proper sleep routine with the little one, consider waking up a little earlier. You will find that taking the first 30 - 60 minutes of the day to just think does wonders for my mental outlook.

Take a few minutes to have a cup of coffee or tea and write down what you need to do for the day or maybe do absolutely nothing. If you want, write down any tasks you have to do earlier and prioritize when you can complete them. This will set you off to a great start of the day.

July 24
Scheduling is Key

As a mother things most often never go as planned. However knowing what to expect can help keep you motivated and focused for the most part, which is why it's important to know your daily schedule and stick with it as much as you possibly can. Having a schedule in place can make it much easier to keep on track and stay productive during the day regardless of the distractions.

July 25
Control Incoming Demands

Children can be a very powerful distraction that can easily take your focus away. It seems that they have a request every 30 seconds. However, you must embrace the fact that your family comes first. The best thing to do here is to try your best to teach your children to ask for things one at a time and also (if age permits) show them how to do things on their own.

If you are doing something very important and it's not a life and death request from your child, try to defer it until you complete the task. Your time can be well spent by teaching your kids to take care of a few things themselves when they ask for something.

July 26
You are not a Robot

Even robots need time to recharge their batteries. And as much as we mothers try to have everything figured out, it's impossible to do it all alone. So find time to recharge your batteries, rejuvenate and reset today.

July 27
It's a Matter of Priorities

Sometimes it's just impossible to accomplish everything on your list in a given day. From changing those dirty diapers every other hour to running those school errands.

There will be those days where everything wrong will happen thereby eating up your time. So when you plan out your day, make sure to complete your most important tasks first - that way you create time to tackle those unforeseen circumstances when they creep up.

July 28
Organize Your Day

As a mother, staying on track can be extremely difficult. So it is important to take a few minutes in the morning to organize your day. Organizing your day can help you stay productive and motivated.

There is nothing more discouraging than having to waste valuable time because you failed to plan ahead. Taking a few minutes to plan ahead and organize how you want to spend your day can help to keep things right on track.

July 29
Think Outside the Box

Balancing work, motherhood, and all the different life challenges can sometimes seem impossible for us mothers. However remember just because things may seem difficult doesn't mean it's impossible.

There is always a way out of every situation and we just need to take a step back and look for other ways of doing things beyond the norm.

July 30
Planning is Key

You know how the saying goes; "*if you fail to plan, then plan to fail*". And yes "mum brain" is a real thing. With so many activities taking over our day to day lives, planning can help guide and stop us from getting those brainfarts.

Without an action plan, you won't be able to move toward your goals efficiently. A plan of action will provide you with a step-by-step guideline for moving toward each of your goals. With an action plan in hand, you can complete necessary tasks every day that are needed to achieve your goals.

Plan for the next day the night before, write those tasks down in a notebook, break your big goal into smaller, more manageable steps and work on them daily.

July 31
Avoid Social Distractions

Social distractions have become even more enhanced thanks to the multitude of social media platforms that are available at our disposal today. Unfortunately, with so many choices it is too often easy for us to spend hours of our time on the networks rather than working on the things that we set out to accomplish.

When you create a routine, you want to be sure to attach a time frame to your plans to help you avoid being distracted by the pull of social media until you complete your tasks. When you aren't distracted by social platforms and other unplanned activities you can better manage your time throughout the day. To help you stay on track, use social media as a reward for being focused and accomplishing what you set out to do during the day.

August

August 1
Happy New Month

Hey mama, welcome to another new month. As you begin this new month, I want you to step into it with a positive mindset. Because the way you think can impact how you feel. So today I want you to make this promise to yourself.

"I am worthy of all the love and happiness that comes to me this month"

Remember those words as you go through this month and remind yourself of that each time you are feeling a little low.

August 2
Break Things Down

One great way to improve on your time management is to break down your bigger tasks into smaller ones. When you break complex tasks down into smaller pieces, it becomes easier to comprehend and follow.

For example, instead of trying to clean the entire house all at once, you could decide to focus on the bedroom only one day, the living room another day and the kitchen another time. It doesn't have to be completed all at one time.

August 3
Set Boundaries

Are you overextending yourself? Then it's time to learn to say no. If you want to be able to manage your time effectively, then you need to learn how to set boundaries.

You cannot be there for everyone and every activity especially if it isn't important or necessary to be there.

People can't read minds, so it is your job to set appropriate boundaries when necessary. Make sure that you communicate your limits in a polite, yet direct manner to ensure that you can have the time you need to work on essential tasks. You cannot always be available for everyone when they need you and that's ok.

August 4
Create Lists

Writing down everything that you need to accomplish and remember throughout the day makes it easier for you to perform your daily tasks.

Trying to remember everything that you need to achieve during the day can drain your energy. By creating lists, you eliminate the need to make an effort memorizing and remembering everything that you have to do.

August 5
Account for Good Distractions

Distractions are an obvious time-killer. There will always be distractions that get the best of you, no matter how hard you try to avoid them.

However, no one can work for hours on end, and stay productive at the same time - we all need breaks. Try to block out some downtime every day. This might mean setting aside a few minutes to take a short walk, grab a cup of coffee, or find some other stress management activities that you can do.

Managing your time requires discipline, planning, and a healthy attitude. However, if you get it right, you will start to notice improved productivity and lower levels of stress.

August 6
Happiness First

You are already doing so much every single day trying to make everyone else happy. Remember to find the time to be patient and kind with yourself too. Because at the end of the day a happy mother equals happy children.

August 7
Keep a Notebook & Pen Handy

Try to keep a notebook with yourself at all times. As long as you are not driving or doing something dangerous, it is best to write down your random thoughts in a notebook. This is a good way to decide what you can prioritize. Plus writing down your ideas can be a powerful tool in managing time effectively.

August 8
Stop Multitasking

It can be incredibly tempting to want to try and take care of everything at once. And I get it, it can be unavoidable as a mother sometimes. However, it has been proven that multitasking just doesn't work.

If you think that you can efficiently juggle changing diapers, cooking, cleaning, laundry at the same time without losing your productivity, you're fooling yourself.

If you want to increase your productivity, you need to focus on one task at a time. So if you can, try and focus on what's important first like attending to the baby and worry about that laundry later.

August 9
Avoid Giant To Do Lists

When you are creating your to-do list, it can be easy to get overzealous and fill it with a dozen or more tasks that you most likely won't be able to complete. If you can only finish half of your to-do list at the end of the day, it can lead to you feeling overwhelmed. So try not to cramp your day with too many things to do as this could quickly leave you feeling overwhelmed and lose your momentum.

August 10
Focus on What's Important

Today I want you to forget about the number of things that need your attention and focus on what needs the most attention first. Perhaps those dishes in the sink could wait till later, perhaps those toys can be parked later. Focus on one thing at a time and don't overwhelm yourself with everything at once.

August 11
Plan the Night Before

Spending just 15 minutes before you go to bed creating and prioritizing your to-do list for the next day will give you a head start the following day. After you create your to-do list, spend a few minutes marking the tasks that are important to serve as a reminder of what needs to be done and push you forward in achieving your goals.

August 12
Reorganize Your Time

Most people struggle with time management because they don't plan for distractions and unexpected events, which can lead to the feeling of being overwhelmed, resulting in procrastination. If you can reorganize your activities around time, you will find that you can still accomplish all the activities that you planned to get done for the day.

August 13
Stay Focused

The last thing you want to do is spend time creating a routine and let it fall by the wayside because you've lost focus. It takes a lot of focus to make your routine a reality. When you wake up in the mornings with a plan you need to develop a focused mindset toward your plan so that nothing distracts you.

Too many people develop routines but don't remain focused on sticking to it. So at the end of the day they have their plans in hand, but allow any and every activity to steal their focus and attention.

If you want to improve your time management skills and increase your productivity as a mother, then you have to be focused and determined to stick to the plan you've made for the day.

August 14
Learn to Delegate

Learning to delegate is extremely beneficial to your overall productivity. Even if this means leaving your child with a nanny, childminder, or at daycare for 1 day a week. It can help free up some of your time and allow you to focus on you.

August 15
Don't Overthink Things

Overthinking can be extremely energy draining and time consuming. So if you are the type of mother that always thinks about the worst case scenario or expects things to always go wrong, then that kind of anxiety can paralyze you and drain you mentally. When you catch yourself having these kinds of thoughts, take a deep breath, and ask yourself what the worst thing that can happen is, then focus on how to deal with it.

August 16
Avoid Procrastination

Falling into a habit of procrastination only makes your tasks more difficult when it's time to complete them. Procrastinating just makes you more stressed because you have to rush things to meet the deadlines that you set for yourself. Procrastination will also cause you to produce low-quality results.

If you begin your tasks at the earliest possible time, you can take more time to complete them without having to finish them in a short amount of time.

Also, when you can finish a task before its deadline, it gives you even more time to sit back, relax and replenish your energy.

August 17
Perfection Doesn't Exist

There is no such thing as the perfect mother. However you can work on becoming the best mother you can possibly be.

One of the ways to improve productivity and manage your time better is to avoid being a perfectionist and assign a time frame to each activity. Set a deadline for yourself and be ruthless in not allowing any changes to be made.

August 18
Hire a Cleaner

Wouldn't it be great to have someone else clean the house that isn't you? Your house is your sanctuary and the state of your house can impact how you feel. If you feel like the house is in need of some TLC, it's ok to hire some help and give yourself a little break.

Get a cleaner to come in and deep clean the house (even if it's once a month). And no, that doesn't make you a bad mother. If anything it makes you a good mother for realising that the house needs to be cleaned and acting towards it. This can help towards freeing up more time for yourself.

August 19
Get Meal Prepping

Another great way to stay organised and manage your time effectively is to prepare your meals in advance. Think of a day when you have more free time, and use that day to cook as many of your meals in advance and preserve them in the fridge.

That way you don't have to cook meals from scratch every single day and can easily pop them in the microwave. This is going to save you so much time and even money having to eat out all the time or order takeout.

August 20
Set a Morning Routine

Having a morning routine can help you gain motivation to propel you into the rest of your day. Knowing what to expect will help you make it through your day.

Changes in your routine can make it difficult to think clearly and have a productive day. However, doing the same general activities in the same order can help you get going. And don't worry if your routine doesn't always go as planned but try working on one anyway.

~ Part 7 - Dealing with Sleep Deprivation ~

Sleep - The golden "S" word that we mothers crave for but never properly get. Whether it be waking up multiple times every hour breastfeeding a newborn or staying up late wondering when your teenager will be home, sleep deprivation is something that mothers struggle with and probably one of the biggest contributing factors to our elevated stress levels.

Let's face it, the only way you will be able to get a proper good night's sleep is if you can get the baby to sleep too. As much as we cannot determine the sleep patterns of our children, there are a few things we can do to make the process smoother for both us and our babies.

Some advocate letting babies "cry it out," while others believe in meeting baby's needs around the clock. Still others support co-sleeping, while the crib camp points to the advantages of a baby having his or her own room.

Here are some tips for helping your baby sleep.

For young babies, especially newborns, the lights, open space, and cold (relative to the womb) temperatures can be overwhelming. Swaddling, or wrapping your baby closely in blankets, can go a long way to helping a baby feel secure enough to sleep.

Fans or white noise devices can be very helpful for promoting baby's sleep. Some parents use an air purifier, or even a radio set on static. Pretty much anything that makes a steady hum and does not pose any risk to baby's safety will work.

Baby does not have to sleep in a crib or bed right off the bat. As long as it's safe, there's no "wrong" place for a baby to sleep. If the baby sleeps well on a blanket on the living room floor, great!

Try varying how you put the baby to sleep. Some experts note that this keeps babies from expecting a particular action - rocking, singing, nursing - in order to fall asleep and fall back asleep. So it's recommended that you vary your methods for putting the baby to sleep.

If babies do not get a lot of cuddling, interaction, touch, and a certain amount of peace and quiet, they may look to have those needs met at night. Try to satisfy your baby's needs for closeness and touch during the day, and you may find that he or she rests more peacefully at night.

August 21
It's Only a Phase

No mother will tell you they haven't dealt with sleep deprivation especially when you have a very young child. The best thing you can do for yourself is try sleeping when they sleep, get in as many naps as you can, and try not to spend that free time tidying up the house or doing the laundry (those can wait). Look after yourself, treat yourself and find support wherever you can. And the good news is, this is only a phase and will soon pass away.

August 22
Baby Sleep Issues?

Baby not getting the required sleep each night? So we all know the rules of your child needing to get a certain number of hours of sleep every single night. Now these are rules that should act as guidelines.

And rules are not particularly created to suit every single child and their individual needs. For example they say by 1 your child should be getting 12-14 hours of sleep a day. What if yours only gets 10 because they are teething, or feeling unwell? Should you then beat yourself up or feel like a failure of a mother? Absolutely not. Every child is different and as long as your child is happy and healthy, you have nothing to worry about.

August 23
Have the Windows Open

Commonly people make the assumption that they will sleep better if they are warm. While you want your body temperature to be warm though, the ideal surrounds are actually slightly cool. This emulates the way we would have slept in the wild and helps us to better regulate our temperature.

August 24
Create a Schedule

It is proven that a routine will trick your body into falling asleep at a specific time. Try to observe yourself and your kids and what time they go to bed. Create a routine around their bedtime and be sure to complete everything before that time so you too are ready for bed. You can also set an alarm that will tell you that it's time to prepare yourself for bedtime.

That way, you are less likely to forget what time it is and be more successful at implementing a routine. And if you have younger babies, then try as much as you can to sleep when they sleep and work around their routine. In doing so you can avoid being overly sleep deprived.

August 25
Create a Routine

Ok! So this strategy will work best once your child is finally settled into a night time routine. This is your opportunity to finally set a routine for yourself too. Avoid those late nights because not only can this leave you fatigued during the rest of the day but it can make your day more tiring too. So try to establish an early night time routine once your little one starts sleeping through the night.

August 26
Take a Warm Shower

This is one of the most powerful ways to help yourself sleep more deeply. Taking a hot shower just before you go to sleep will not only relax your muscles, it will also trigger your body to produce growth hormone and melatonin, essentially getting you nicely drowsy.

August 27
Have Half an Hour Before Bed

Half an hour before bed, take your phone into another room and leave it there. At the same time, turn off the TV and make a conscious effort to relax and to do something that you will enjoy.

This will help you to unwind and to let go of the stresses of the day. What's more, the lack of bright screens will help you to avoid stimulating the production of cortisol.

August 28
Create a Ritual

A bedtime ritual is an excellent addition to your schedule. A good bedtime ritual is one that allows you to relax, disconnect from the stress of life, and slowly tell your body that it is time to shut down.

Here are a few things you can add to your ritual: Take a bath, go to bed 1 hour before bedtime and read a book, drink herbal tea, listen to calming music, and do some meditation. This will ensure that you have a good night's sleep.

August 29
Set a Comfortable Environment

Don't underestimate the comfort of your bed and pillow and the power of fresh linen. If you are uncomfortable, you will likely have a hard time falling asleep or staying asleep.

Another aspect of comfort is the temperature of the room and the level of noise around. Try sleeping with a fan on or a white noise machine.

Having a constant sound in the room could help you maintain your sleep. If you like essential oils, try a drop of lavender on your pillow, this will help the brain relax.

August 30
Turn Off Devices

This will probably be the most challenging thing to do but also the most impactful, which is to turn off any electronics 1 hour before bedtime. Spend the last hour doing something calming and relaxing. Try to have your device outside the bedroom during the night; this will allow you not to be disturbed during your sleep.

Experts say that the bed should be used for sleep and relaxation. If you work, browse social media or watch TV from your bed, your brain will associate the bed with a zone of activity and will likely be active even when it is bedtime. Train your mind to see your bed as a place to disconnect from the digital world.

August 31
Sleep Like Your Baby

Think about how babies go to sleep. Mom and Dad create a ritual around bedtime. They get a bath, a quiet story, cuddles, comfy clothing, a clean bed, and soft blankets. All of this starts well before bedtime and helps the child calm down, so that when you sit down in bed to read they usually fall asleep fast if not with the first book, then by the third.

You should do the same thing for yourself to help you sleep such as stretching, bathing, applying lotion, dressing for bed, and reading something positive. Bedtime is not the time to read anything upsetting, scary, or even exciting. Use that time to read uplifting or thoughtful poetry, history, or something that keeps your heart rate low.

September

September 1
Go for a Walk

Not long before you're about to go to bed but earlier in the day. This will help you to burn more energy, thus making you more tired when you hit the sack. At the same time, if you take your run outdoors, then you should find that the combination of fresh air and daylight also help you to sleep better as well as to regulate your internal body clock.

September 2
Stop Snoozing

Rather than snooze your alarm clock and try to catch an extra 5 minutes of sleep, start your morning routine earlier when the kids are still asleep. Doing so gives you more time to yourself to make the morning an enjoyable routine rather than one you resent. So try and wake up a little earlier before the kids and spend that time focusing on you.

September 3
Talk to an Expert

Sometimes, sleep problems could be due to more extreme and underlying health issues that need to be dealt with.

If you've tried all you can but are still struggling with sleep, it might be a good idea to consult your doctor or a sleep expert. There are other solutions that they can provide you with to improve your sleep situation.

~ Part 8 - Dealing with Stress & Anxiety ~

September 4
Identify the Root Cause

Stress is one of the biggest problems we face as mothers. Identify what makes you stressful and uneasy. Making a list of your stressful experiences is useful.

Immediately dealing with the issues that you can change, for instance waking up earlier for work in the morning, keeping the house clean, not leaving things till the last minute can also help.

Forget about the issues that you cannot influence like being stuck in a traffic jam or a toddler throwing a tantrum because quite frankly we cannot change these.

September 5
Don't be Too Hard on Yourself

Most of the stress that we experience in our lives is self-induced. If you want to combat stress and eliminate fatigue from your life, then you have to avoid being too hard on yourself. Avoid burning the candle at both ends. Take the time to relax and recharge yourself and avoid working too hard and pushing yourself to the point of extreme exhaustion.

September 6
Declutter Your Mind

When you start to feel completely overwhelmed, it's best to step away from the situation and take a deep breath. Allow your mind to relax and clear itself from stress. Going into something with a clear mind will provide you with the fresh perspective that you need to help you stay motivated and productive.

September 7
Avoid Multitasking

One of the biggest reasons why we end up stressed as mothers is because we try to juggle everything at once. Just because you can doesn't mean you have to. Multitasking can result in a lot of stress and burnout.

Rather than splitting your focus to accomplish numerous tasks, devote your entire focus to the task at hand. Find a quiet place to work and cut out all distractions. Concentrate on one task at a time, only moving on when you've accomplished the task.

September 8
Enjoy the Moment

Being a parent comes with so many responsibilities. And one of these responsibilities is thinking not only about our future but that of your kids. What schools will they go to? What will they grow up to become? Is there enough money to raise them? And the list goes on.

If you want to make continuous progress, it is important that you learn how to live in the present. Not to say you should ignore the future, but dwelling too much about it can overwhelm you, making it extremely tough to work on the current task effectively. Likewise, when you live in the past and continue to remember the setbacks you've experienced, you're unable to take the meaningful action you need to continue to move forward. So try and live today and stop stressing too much about the future.

September 9
Everyday is a Gift

Feeling a little frustrated today? The kids giving you a headache? Well the fact that you are able to read this right now means you are alive. And that's a gift in itself and something you need to be thankful and grateful for.

September 10
Every Child is Different

Feeling frustrated because your baby isn't on solids by 6 months, isn't standing by 1 year or not yet potty trained by 3? Well how about the amazing developments your child has already gone through? Instead of trying to compare with the next mother and how perfect she portrays her child to be, why not appreciate the amazing things your child is already doing and stop stressing over things you have no control over. At the end of the day remember every child is different.

September 11
Practice Visualization

As a mother, visualisation can be a powerful way to avoid that feeling of overwhelm and stress. Visualization is an effective technique for changing your belief and reaching your goals. Your mind can't differentiate between something vividly imagined and real life. Using visualization can provide your subconscious mind with manufactured pieces of evidence that will reinforce positive thinking in your mind.

September 12
Don't Take on Too Much

Often when you are busy, you tend to take on much more than what you can handle at once. The strain of taking on too much can cause you to become stressed and result in you losing focus on what is really important. Always be aware of what your limits are and act accordingly.

September 13
Take a Deep Breathe

Every couple of hours take a 5-minute break and focus on your breathing. Sit up straight, close your eyes, and place your hand on your belly. Slowly inhale through your nose and feel the breath begin in your abdomen and work its way up to the top of your head.

Reverse the process as you exhale through your mouth. Breathing deeply in this manner helps to counter the effects of stress by slowing down your heart rate and lowering your blood pressure.

September 14
Tackle the Problem

Life is full of unexpected, stressful, and difficult periods and events. Whenever these challenging times arise, it is easy to feel overwhelmed, overworked, and overall dissatisfied with your life.

Even more worrisome is that we often ignore these feelings or chalk them up to weakness whenever they arise. To stop the cycle head-on, we must recognize how we are feeling, understand the situation fully, and take active steps to be more compassionate to ourselves and problem-solve our way out of the situation.

September 15
Have Faith

There's nothing more powerful than having faith. Saying a short prayer in times of stress can give you a sense of calm, especially when the situation is one you really have no control over. Studies have shown that people who trust in a higher power have lower blood pressure. Holding a grudge is not good for your health and can affect your blood pressure. so learn to forgive and let go.

September 16
Take that Nap

Self care isn't only bubble baths and some wine. Something as little as taking a nap can have a drastic impact on your emotional and physical well being. A power nap can also help with stress relief and keep you more alert - which is important to us as mothers. So give yourself that power nap whenever you possibly can.

September 17
It's Only Temporal

Baby not latching? Struggling to get any sleep? Dealing with a teething baby? Struggling to balance it all? One thing you must remember is that this is just a phase and it will be over before you know it.

Remind yourself that the stressful event will end sooner or later and look more into the positive sides of things.

At the same time, calm down your emotions and think of the best thing to do rather than take your energy away from what needs to be done.

September 18
Handle the Chaos

A chaotic time is anything that leaves you feeling stressed, overwhelmed, overworked, or chaotic. It does not matter what the situation or event was.

The only thing that matters is how you feel in response to the situation. This can include your actual emotions, as well as how you plan to react to the situation. You owe it to yourself to learn tools to better navigate those times in a healthy and functional manner.

September 19
Stay Focused

Focus on the journey in front of you right now and stop stressing over things that happened last week, yesterday or an hour ago. You cannot control what has already happened but can certainly control what battles you are about to face right in front of you. You got this.

September 20
Your Health is Wealth

The very best thing that you can do for yourself and health is to eat, drink and rest. Stress is easily brought on by not eating and drinking properly. When you don't get the number of hours of sleep that you need each night, you are only setting yourself up for additional stress.

September 21
Forget About Yesterday

Yesterday is history, it's over with. Try not to let your issues from yesterday spoil today. Instead, start each day with a new, positive outlook, telling yourself that today is going to be better.

Starting each day with a fresh slate is the best way to get past previous differences. Holding onto a grudge only hurts yourself.

September 22
Find Time to Rest

As a busy mother, rest might seem like an alien concept. Too often, mums will push aside their personal needs in order to accomplish what it is they set out to do. To keep your motivation and reach your goals, you need to make a point of taking a break during your day.

Depending on your circumstances, this can mean treating yourself to lunch, having a coffee date with a friend, or finding some time to read a few chapters of your book. Make it a point to have some time to rest so that you don't burn out.

September 23
Take a Holiday

Take a holiday. It doesn't have to be a fancy vacation resort. A day at the beach, or an afternoon at the park will do. Just anywhere you can be and not think about the bills, work, or whatever tensions you may have. It's important to take time for yourself, so do it! You'll feel better with a fresh outlook

September 24
Prepare in Advance

One of the best ways to lessen the strain of road rage is to prepare everything the night before. Clothes and even packed lunches should be set the day before to avoid the morning rush. With everything champing at the bit, you'd save plenty of time to do your morning routines, devour a good breakfast and enjoy special moments with the family. Best of all, you can dash out the highway free of traffic congestion.

September 25
Stop Overthinking

It's easy to get sucked into sitting around at home and contemplating life and its challenges. Sometimes with no help from others at all we take on the task of dragging ourselves down.

Train your mind to recognize these periods and do something about it. We all lapse into these moments. It doesn't have to remain so. Break the cycle by doing something fresh as soon as you recognize yourself plunging into this nasty state.

September 26
Get Outside

There's nothing more powerful and refreshing than a breath of fresh air. This is especially common when you are looking after a newborn. Try and take 15 minutes today to just go outside for a walk, breathe in some of that fresh air and relax.

This is a great way to disconnect from all the overwhelm and can do wonders for your mental health. And if you don't have someone to watch after the little one, put them on a stroller and take them along with you. It would do them some good too.

September 27
Give Yourself Some Space

Life is already overwhelming as it is, and for a mother this can feel 1000 times more. So try to allow yourself downtime to breathe and clear your mind.

When you rush from task to task, it can be difficult to appreciate what you're doing and to stay focused and motivated. So do remember to find some time for yourself.

September 28
Stop Striving for Perfection

Most mothers continuously aim for perfectionism, trying to raise perfect kids or trying to do everything perfectly according to the book. The problem with this is that you are continually setting yourself up to fail by setting unrealistic standards for yourself.

One of the most powerful ways you can deal with stress and anxiety in your life is to drop the notion of perfectionism. There is no such thing as a perfect mother, but the important thing is recognizing that your best is good enough.

September 29
Don't Take it Too Seriously

This life is complicated enough as it is, don't add to your stress by taking life and yourself too seriously. If you aim to live a happy and stress-free life, you have to develop a great sense of humor.

It is vital that you learn to laugh at yourself. There is always something funny in every situation that you find yourself in, even the most difficult circumstances. Finding the humor in life will help you feel better and will instantly increase your energy.

September 30
Talk to Someone

We cannot go through the journey of motherhood alone. Sometimes it's a good idea to just talk to someone. Talking to someone you trust can help you manage your stress and increase the amount of energy you have every day. It can also be incredibly therapeutic and help you learn how to manage your stress better.

October

October 1
Happy New Month

Hey mama, welcome to another new month. As you begin this new month, I want you to step into it with a positive mindset. Because the way you think can impact how you feel. So today I want you to make this promise to yourself.

"I am going to take care of myself because taking care of me is taking care of my children"

Remember those words as you go through this month and remind yourself of that each time you are feeling a little low.

October 2
Be Clear About Your Goals

To avoid spreading yourself too thin and avoid excess stress, it is essential that you are clear about what you want to achieve. Start setting clear goals in every area of your life, including personal development, career, finances, health, and relationships. Knowing exactly what you need to do to achieve your goals will keep you from becoming overly stressed and exhausted.

October 3
Forgive Yourself

If you always feel guilty about things that you've done in the past, you will only increase your levels of exhaustion and stress. You have to learn to forgive yourself for your past mistakes if you want to live a life free of stress and fatigue.

Creating healthy personal boundaries is one of the most powerful ways that you can prevent stress in your life and eliminate fatigue.

October 4
Stop Trying to Control Everything

There are going to be things that come up in your life that you simply can't control. If you want to live a happy, stress-free, and high energy life, then you need to focus your energy on those things in your life that you can control and learn to let go of the things that you can't control.

October 5
It's all for the Best

We often feel stressed and frustrated when we fail to get what we want. This should not be the case because this may sometimes be an amazing stroke of better opportunities.

Remember everything happens for a reason and we cannot change what we cannot control. So stop stressing yourself over things and recognize it's all for the best.

October 6
Connect with Nature

Nature is always very relaxing, which is why it's a perfect way to deal with stress. You don't even need anyone with you most of the time since being alone in the woods surrounded by nothing but the trees and the many sounds of wildlife (hopefully not dangerous ones) living in that ecosystem can be extremely calming.

It will help you clear your mind and relieve any stress that you could've built up over the course of the week. It might be hard at first to just put every electronic device you have on you away, and indulge in nature's beauty.

October 7
Eliminate the Junk

It may seem like a no brainer for some and a surprise for others, but stress is highly associated with clutter. While living with depression can often increase the risk of clutter, studies have shown that the more clutter you are surrounded in, the more stressful an experience you will have.

Living in a clean environment is a surefire way to begin eliminating stress from your life. Whether it's just tidying up more regularly or doing a major overhaul of your clutter, the moral of the story is the same. Less mess equals less stress.

October 8
Stop Scaring Yourself

Fear is the most common culprit behind stress and anxiety. When you refuse to allow yourself to become scared you can effectively remove the primary reason for your anxiety.

When you eliminate fear from your life, you can gain more control of your body's emergency response system and take control of your anxiety.

October 9
Retreat from Social Media

Going dark on social media seems sometimes like you are punishing those around you or being weird. However, it is actually healthy to disconnect every once in a while and allow yourself to fully experience the range of your surroundings without having technology distracting you from the world around you.

Social media can often be a mentally, emotionally, and physically draining experience forcing us to compare our lives to the lives of other people. However, studies have proven that there is no faster way to low self esteem than to compare ourselves to other people. So give yourself a break from social media especially if it's contributing to your stress.

October 10
Distract Yourself

Most anxiety attacks are caused and fueled by anxious thoughts. When you can distract your attention, you can effectively prevent anxious thoughts from taking over.

As you prevent your thoughts from turning anxious, you can also put an end to voluntary anxiety attacks.

October 11
Ask for Help

For some reason, one of the hardest things to do is to ask for help. This seems ridiculous, considering we are such a communal species. So why is it that it seems so impossible sometimes to ask for help?

Too many people feel that they have to go it alone, especially mothers. Maybe we have had an experience in the past that made us feel as if we had nobody to rely on. Maybe it seems as if there isn't anyone out there who actually cares what we are going through. Maybe we have been disappointed one too many times by others and we feel that the only person we can rely on to do something right is ourselves.

Nevertheless, don't be afraid to ask for help when you need it. And if you find yourself taking on more than you can bear, let it be known. Don't hide it or keep it to yourself as this can increase stress levels.

October 12
Identify Bad Habits

All of us have a vice. Some of us are smokers, some of us are over-eaters, some of us spend too much money. The unfortunate fact is that most of us are usually trying to find a way to cope with the stresses that creep up on us during daily life. Maybe we aren't strong enough to handle them on our own.

At least, that's what we tell ourselves. What we need most during times like these is a good support system. We need people on our side telling us that we can keep going even when we feel we are destined to fail.So find ways to address these situations in a more positive way rather than by falling back on a vice that is only going to hurt you in the long run.

October 13
Avoid Processed Foods

When we eat processed foods, the levels of stress in our bodies are likely to rise. It is dangerous because our cortisol levels will rise exponentially through the consumption of unhealthy and processed foods.

By consuming foods that will cause our stress levels to rise, whether we are aware of it or not, we are subjecting ourselves to major health issues, not only physically, but potentially emotionally. It is therefore important to try and remain conscious of the effects of each of the choices that we make.

October 14
The Power of Taking a Break

It's important to allow ourselves chances to relax throughout the day and try not to guilt trip ourselves for needing some down time. Especially for us mothers where being busy all the time appears to be a new normal.

It's almost as if not doing anything is a waste of time you could be spending on the laundry, cleaning the house, etc. Recognise that it's ok to take a break and do absolutely nothing because doing too much would in fact slow down your productivity and burn you out that much faster.

October 15
Redirect Your Feelings

One of the most important things you can do to reduce stress is to learn how to redirect your thoughts and feelings. When you find yourself getting overwhelmed by the triggering situations that you face in day to day life, redirection is crucial in maintaining your peace of mind.

And it is something that everyone can do. To begin, you have to become mindful of the things that you are allowing yourself to think. So try and redirect those negative thoughts into positive ones.

October 16
Take Care of Your Body

It is far easier to avoid being overwhelmed by stress if you are doing everything you can to maintain your physical health. Physical and mental health are often closely related. When we are feeling sick and stressed out, this can sometimes be because we are deficient in certain vitamins or because we are not doing everything we can to stay on top of our physical health and well-being.

Not only that, but staying on top of a strong health and fitness regimen can promote chemical changes in your body which makes it physically easier to maintain a better outlook on life overall. By taking care of your body, you will find it far easier to maintain a better mood.

October 17
Calm Yourself

Being able to calm yourself down helps to shut off the mechanism in your brain that causes anxiety attacks and ends your body's stress response. The more you can calm yourself down, the faster you can stop the anxiety attack and start to feel better. A sure way to end, control, and prevent stress is to find out ways to calm yourself down.

October 18
Build a Support Network

Perhaps one of the most organic ways to remain stress free is to build a support network. When you have people in your corner who are willing to help you out, it helps to stay motivated and feel positive, even when things seem rough. People all over the world know the power of other human beings being a part of their circle. It is something unrivaled.

We have friends for a reason. They are there to help us stay lifted when things are difficult and to give us someone to vent to when we feel like we need a listening ear. So look into mum groups, facebook communities where you can mingle with other mothers. This will help you beat some of that stress and recognize you are not alone on this journey.

October 19
Expose Yourself to Fear

Even though it can be terrifying, if you want to overcome your fears, then you just have to face them. Whether it be separation anxiety from your child because you have to go back to work, or struggling to get them to eat. Sit down and define the worst-case scenario of the unknown outcome, and realize that the worst scenario rarely happens. Doing this you'll start to notice that each time you do the scary thing, it gets a little bit easier.

October 20
You Cannot Fix it All

When things in your life seem out of control, you will feel like nothing seems right.

It would make you feel so overwhelmed and you won't even feel sure about how you can pull yourself out of that black hole you found yourself in. Just the same as anything that you attempt to resolve in your life, it's essential to understand your state of mind.

Never try to solve your entire problems all at once because it could result in even more stress than you bargained for. Take it one step at a time and only focus on what you can control.

~ Part 9 - Healthy Living & Boosting Your Immunity ~

Research has shown that problems such as stress, fatigue, anxiety and depression are directly triggered by the way we feel inside. For example, when you have a headache, you need to take paracetamol to heal you inside so you can feel good on the outside.

If your internal health isn't right, your overall physical and mental health will equally be impacted. So it is essential that we look after our internal health as mothers so we can avoid a lot of the external difficulties that we struggle with.

So in the next few days we are going to be diving straight into healthy living tips, tricks and hacks that can guide you towards your journey of a healthier happier you. And nutrition isn't only for mothers but also for your kids.

Disclaimer: Always speak to a qualified nutritionist or expert before you embark on any drastic health and lifestyle changes. These tips should be used as a guide and for information purposes.

October 21
It Starts with the Kids

To become a better person, children need to be emotionally, mentally and physically healthy. No parent would want her child to get sick, so making sure that they are healthy is really important. Offer your child with the best nutrition to prevent sickness from taking place.

Feeding young children with a balanced diet could be very hard, specifically when they belong to the group of fussy eaters. The trick to keep in mind is that you do not need to stick with a particular food item to help your child get some nutrients his body needs. For instance, meat would provide your child with protein, yet he may also acquire protein from chickpeas or nuts.

October 22
Positive Affirmation of the Day

Today is a day of positive affirmation. As you go through this day, repeat these words to yourself each time you find yourself drifting apart or feeling a little low.

"I am looking forward to a healthy future because I take care of my body now".

October 23
Don't Forget About Breakfast

If you are going to skip any meals today, just make sure it isn't breakfast. As a mother it's very easy to feed the children and everyone else but us. So when you are making breakfast for your little one(s) today, remember to include yourself on the menu.

Eating a healthy and balanced breakfast is the key to starting your day out right. Food is energy, so by eating in the morning and choosing the right types of foods, you will remain focused on your daily tasks and goals. Even when you feel pressed for time, have a go-to meal that will give you the nutrition you need to start your day off right.

October 24
Get Energized

If you lack energy, how could you even begin to look after your little one? So it's important to think about things that energize you and give you the necessary boost to get moving. Whether this means having some breakfast first thing in the morning, getting a workout, staying hydrated, taking a multivitamin, going for a walk or taking a power nap, be sure to get all that energy in there, so you are physically able to care for your little one.

October 25
Nourish Your Body

There is no better feeling than nourishing the body with the right nutrients it needs. When your body is properly nourished, you start to look good, feel good and happier. And when you start to feel great and happy, that energy is equally transferred to your children. So remember to nourish yourself today with a nice healthy meal that can provide your body with all the nutrients it needs.

October 26
Exercise is Essential

And when we talk about exercise this doesn't mean signing up for a gym membership or running everyday like you are practicing for a marathon. Start off small. Exercise is not only great for your body, but for your mental health as well! Remember every little helps.

October 27
Stay Hydrated

Whilst writing this, I just realised I haven't had enough water today! *"quickly sips on some water"*. Ok much better. So back to the topic of staying hydrated. It can be very difficult not only for busy mamas but individuals as a whole to stay hydrated.

One way to overcome this and keep hydrated is by filling a bottle of water in the morning and keeping it next to you - be it at your desk at work or somewhere close to you at home. Not only is this a great way to track how much water you are drinking, it keeps you hydrated throughout the day. And if you aren't a fan of drinking plain water, try squeezing in a fruit of your choice to give the water some flavour. The more hydrated you are, the happier and healthier you feel.

October 28
Positive Affirmation of the Day

Today is a day of positive affirmation. As you go through this day, repeat these words to yourself each time you find yourself drifting apart or feeling a little low.

"I will eat healthy, nutritious, energy-giving and balanced foods that benefit my entire body.

October 29
Maintain a Stable Blood Sugar

Our western diets do nothing to promote healthy and stable blood sugar levels, and every time we experience a drop in our blood sugar we can start to feel anxious. To maintain your blood sugar levels, you need to incorporate plenty of proteins and healthy fats into your diet and avoid sugar and refined carbohydrates.

October 30
Have a Blender Handy

There's never been an easier way to eat more fruits and vegetables than blending them together and drinking it up. So when you are having one of those days where you just can't seem to figure out what to have for breakfast or just don't have the time to whip something up, a quick smoothie always does the trick.

You can even blend vegetables together and make some soup. And this is super amazing for the kids too.

October 31
Have a Game Plan

You wouldn't go on a trip without a map, be it a paper one or a GPS device, so why would you commit to a healthier lifestyle without a plan? Just like you make up a shopping list before heading to the grocery store, you should also map out the path to your goal.

It's just not feasible to go about an overhaul of your life without a game plan. What are you going to eat? What exercise program will you follow? What will you be giving up in search of a healthier you? There are so many things to consider before beginning your journey, and mapping it all out is a great way to organize your thoughts.

Remember that failure to plan is planning to fail, and you want this new lifestyle to be a success!

November

November 1
Happy New Month

Hey mama, welcome to another new month. As you begin this new month, I want you to step into it with a positive mindset. Because the way you think can impact how you feel. So today I want you to make this promise to yourself.

"I am amazing in the eyes of my children and that's all that matters"

Remember those words as you go through this month and remind yourself of that each time you are feeling a little low.

November 2
Stock Your Refrigerator

Is there anything worse than a growling stomach with nothing ready and prepared? Although it is far easier to jump online and order take out, you should always keep your kitchen stocked with nutritious food!

You don't need a large amount of food to be able to whip up some quick meals. All it takes is a basic mixture of fresh and frozen veggies, and simple cooking skills. Voila! A hearty, healthy meal is never more than a few minutes away. Be specific with the items you purchase from the grocery store. Quick and easy does not have to be terrible for you.

November 3
Avoid Sugary Drinks

While it's common knowledge that our bodies are made up of mostly water, and therefore we should continuously be drinking it, there are reasons as to why we should actually avoid sugary drinks altogether.

Whenever you drink your calories, be it in the form of soda or an alcoholic beverage, your brain gets thrown off track. In addition to consuming more calories, drinking this stuff can also have some nasty, long-term effects on your overall health. Start cutting back slowly and switching to water. The more you do it, the less you'll crave it. It won't be long before you're drinking a big liter of water everyday instead of all of those excess calories!

November 4
Positive Affirmation of the Day

Today is a day of positive affirmation. As you go through this day, repeat these words to yourself each time you find yourself drifting apart or feeling a little low.

"I feel good, my body feels good, and I radiate nothing but good feelings".

November 5
Yummy Fruits & Vegetables

Remember when your parents told you to eat your fruits and vegetables? Well, they were right, and it's always a good time to bring them back into your diet. Not only are they full of nutrients that your body absolutely needs, but they add beautiful colors to your daily meals.

It also makes us feel fuller, which is what's needed to keep us away from all of those bad foods we love to snack on.

So, the next time you make a plate of food, make sure that most of it is full of veggies and some fruit. Think of bright green broccoli, beautiful strawberries, and hearty kale!

November 6
Cardio is Essential

The research has been done, and the results have been out for quite some time: cardiovascular workouts are imperative to a long, healthy life. Whether it's a daily walk or intense run on the treadmill, there are so many benefits to getting your heart rate up! It helps lower your chances of heart disease and diabetes. Both of which are life threatening and far too common in our society.

By committing to a daily cardio workout, be it big or small, you can lower your chances of those, and many other illnesses. Talk about a small change with a big, long-lasting impact! Plus this would leave you looking and feeling good mama.

November 7
Celebrate Small Victories

Not a single person out there goes from unhealthy to perfectly fit, with all positive habits, overnight. It's not possible. What is possible is creating small changes that lead to small victories. Those small victories will eventually graduate into larger ones. The decision to commit to a healthy lifestyle is a huge undertaking.

First off, you should start your new journey off with a celebration. Get excited about taking the first big step toward a better and healthier you.

Next, make sure you are realistic with yourself and know that there will be times that you will have to force yourself to get up, to eat healthy, and sometimes it can be a real struggle. No matter how small something is, you should always take time to congratulate yourself for working so hard!

November 8
Positive Affirmation of the Day

Today is a day of positive affirmation. As you go through this day, repeat these words to yourself.

"I will care for myself by exercising, eating right, and getting enough sleep".

November 9
Don't forget the Probiotics

Intestinal health is just as important as physical health. We consume both good and bad bacteria in the foods that we eat, and it's important to keep it all balanced. One of the side effects of a buildup of bad bacteria is gastroenteritis. This can cause nausea, vomiting, diarrhea, and in extreme cases, hospitalization due to dehydration. Probiotics can both cure and prevent this nasty infection.

There are many ways to take probiotics nowadays, too. The most common form is yogurt. Many people choose this option to get their daily dose of probiotics because of the taste, and because it's considered to be a healthy snack. If you're not into the taste and texture of yogurt, however, you can also go with a supplement. There are many different brands on the market to choose from.

November 10
Avoid Caffeine

You can't underestimate the relationship between caffeine and anxiety. Caffeinated beverages amp up our nervous systems, getting us ready for a fight. Try to reduce your intake of caffeine gradually to avoid any withdrawal symptoms. Within a few weeks, your anxiety symptoms should start to decrease making you feel amazing.

November 11
The Power of Zip Lock Bags

There's never an excuse to not make healthy, pre-planned meals - thanks to Zip-Lock bags. Not only do they come in a variety of sizes, but many of them allow you to write on the outside of the packaging, which makes meal prep even easier!

When you're stocking up on good food at the store, make sure to swing by the section that carries foil and plastic wrap. You'll find a large selection of Zip-Lock bags that are perfect for portioning out your meals!

With these on hand, both at your job and at home, you can say goodbye to inhaling bags of potato chips, and hello to healthy, portioned out meals. They're easy to stack in your cupboard, fit nicely in a lunch pail, and can even go in your purse.

November 12
Stick to healthy Habits

One of the best ways to start your day off right is to develop healthy morning habits and start your day off on a positive note. When you can train yourself to develop healthy habits, you will find that your energy levels through the day have increased dramatically.

November 13
It's all about Portion Control

Before you grab a plate, remember that quality is more important than quantity. Pay attention to what you're about to consume, not how much. Just because you're eating a salad, doesn't mean it's necessarily good for you. Dressings can contain simple sugars, chemicals, and heavy fat content.

In reality, eating too much of anything is bound to make you feel bad, regardless of how good it tastes. Just think about the last time you ate a few too many slices of pizza! So try to ease up on the portions and mix a healthy proportion of carbohydrates, protein and vegetables.

November 14
Consume Healthy Carbs

Whenever you hear the word 'carbs,' chances are, your outlook is less than favorable. After all, just look at all those high protein/low carb diets. However our bodies actually need carbs - especially as busy mothers, always on the move. Without energy, you would have no energy to look after those little ones. The problem isn't carbs, it's the type of carbs that we are consuming. You can switch bad carbs for good carbs such as; oatmeal, whole grains, and brown rice. These types of carbs are called Complex Carbohydrates. Have you ever heard the saying, "Your eyes are bigger than your stomach?"

It's easy to overestimate how much food you really need to consume in order to feel full and satisfied, which is why it's important to go out of your way to monitor your portion sizes.

November 15
How was Your Last Meal?

What was the last thing you ate? Was it healthy? Was it a cheat meal? Did you even bother to check? As mothers we are always on the move and sometimes we quickly grab a bite without thinking twice about it.

However it is important to incorporate some healthy foods into our diet. Healthy eating can extend your life and open you up to new levels of personal satisfaction. Eating healthy will positively affect every other aspect of your life and make you a happier person overall.

November 16
Positive Affirmation of the Day

Today is a day of positive affirmation. As you go through this day, repeat these words to yourself.

"I am strong and feel good about myself and how healthy I am".

November 17
Struggling to Get the Kids Healthy?

There is nothing more difficult than having to raise kids who are fussy eaters or only want to eat chips for breakfast, lunch and dinners. Why not think of alternative ways to get them the required nutrition like blending their fruits into ice lollies or turning them into smoothies? Perhaps a supplement in their Milk could help? Don't beat yourself over it, just find alternative ways to get those results.

November 18
Watch the Portions

We all know that breakfast is the most important meal of the day. However, you also want to try to avoid overeating in the morning because this will only make you feel sluggish and slow you down for the rest of the day. It's best if you eat a small serving of an antioxidant smoothie, or an egg on a muffin, or a small bowl of berries or a piece of fruit, or even some yogurt with nuts sprinkled on top. Keep it healthy and balanced.

November 19
Positive Affirmation of the Day

Today is a day of positive affirmation. As you go through this day, repeat these words to yourself.

"I will breathe nice and deeply, exercise regularly, and feed my body healthy, nutritious foods".

November 20
Plan Things Ahead

How many nights have you spent laying on the couch, scrolling through the television and thinking about everything that you have to do the following day? Take a little time to plan ahead. Prepare your lunch and snacks, set up the coffee maker for the morning, and lay out your clothes. Then watch as everything comes together so much easier the next morning.

November 21
Get Your Vitamins

Now of course, the best way to get more vitamins is directly through our diet and the foods we consume. However, in an ideal world, most people either don't like to eat healthy foods or simply don't have the time to make healthy foods. So if you can get your nutrients from your diet then that's great but if you need a little extra help, then supplements can't hurt.

November 22
A Little Yoga Won't Hurt

Practicing yoga is a healthy way for you to get physical exercise, as well as improving your mindfulness. It is an exercise that you can choose to do at home, or you can join a local class with a friend. Joining a class with a friend will help to keep you motivated to continue your yoga practice. Plus this is a great way to get your mind off screaming kids and focus on just you.

November 23
You Got This

You've been through an incredible journey so far that so many will never understand. You didn't come this far to give up. Keep going and do it for those little people that matter the most to you and are looking up to you.

November 24
Take Photographs

This is a great tactic if you want to lose weight. But you can also use it for other goals as well. Take a selfie of how you look right now and print it off. Post this picture somewhere you visit regularly. Then find some photographs of people that are in the shape that you want to be in.

Post these by the side of your photograph. If you need motivation to continue with your diet plan for example just take a look at your picture and the picture of the person who is in the shape that you want to be in. It will get you excited and help to boost your motivation.

November 25
Mistakes are Ok

Mistakes mean you take the fall. If you do something wrong, accidentally or on purpose for the sake of curiosity, you've made a mistake. Now it's up to you to learn from it or avoid it. A mistake must be admitted before you can ever learn something from it. So if you find yourself drifting away from eating healthy meals, be willing to admit that you've made a mistake and take the initiative to adjust things.

November 26
Positive Affirmation of the Day

Today is a day of positive affirmation. As you go through this day, repeat these words to yourself.

"I am incredibly grateful for the air I'm breathing, the water I have access to, and the food in my refrigerator"

November 27
It's All in Your Thoughts

Did you know that your thoughts have the power to control some events in your life? Well, that is right. Your thoughts are really powerful and they can greatly affect your life in so many ways. What you think can help you create the reality that you experience. Whether such experience is positive or negative, all of these things are determined by your thoughts.

Therefore it is important for you to master the art of controlling your thoughts. As you come to realize that your thoughts are creating your own reality and begin to control your thoughts, you will be able to greatly attract in your life the things which you intend to experience and achieve.

November 28
Set Goals

This can help with planning and maintaining a healthy diet and exercise regime. Do this in the morning or the night before for the preceding day.

Write your goals out in full because it will help to keep them uppermost in your mind. It is recommended that you keep a journal and use this for your daily goal writing. You can also record your experiences along the way and what you have achieved so far. This will help motivate you towards accomplishing even more in the future.

November 29
Turn it Off

The convenience that cell phones have added to our lives can actually be a double-edged sword. We depend on them so much it seems we can't live without them.

This increased accessibility means not only can our loved ones reach us at any time, but so can work. However, giving yourself a break from using that cell phone is actually healthier than you think. Even if it's an hour each day where you simply don't check your phone. Try it and watch how healthy this can be for you.

November 30
Yes You Can Do It

To effectively push yourself forward and embrace challenges, you have to develop a can-do attitude.

Doing this requires a commitment to yourself that you will do whatever it takes to become more disciplined and that you will strive for what matters most to you despite all odds. So be strong today mama and believe you can do whatever you set your mind to it.

~ Part 10 - Managing Finances, Money & Going Back to Work ~

Financial strain is one of the biggest causes of stress, anxiety, and depression in most people in society and that can be worse for a mother trying to balance things out with raising children, going back to work, and trying to make ends meet.

Although some mothers are comfortable relying on their partners fully for financial support, some mothers may not have that luxury or may prefer working to bring something to the table. And for single mothers with no one to rely on, these pressures can seem even worse. Not forgetting the stay at home mums too who equally have to deal with this strain.

Going back to work for some mothers has also proven to be therapeutic because they don't get to lose themselves, they can mingle with other adults which is a great distraction from the kids, and they can contribute to the household financially. Plus being out of work or taking gaps from work too long can affect your chances of getting back into employment in the future.

Unfortunately, with raising kids there's always going to be a problem of balancing work and being a mother whether you decide to go back to work or not.

So in the next few days we are going to be exploring some tips that could help minimize the financial pressures and strain that come with being a mother.

December

December 1
Happy New Month

Hey mama, welcome to another new month. As you begin this new month, I want you to step into it with a positive mindset. Because the way you think can impact how you feel. So today I want you to make this promise to yourself.

"I am creating the best life for my kids, so they will never lack anything"

Remember those words as you go through this month and remind yourself of that each time you are feeling a little low.

December 2
Set Financial Goals

The first step to keeping track of your finances is setting financial goals. You should understand how to prioritize your financial goals so that you'll stay pleased and financially stable as you juggle with life. Set an amount monthly for food, water and shelter as these are your primary needs. Make sure to prioritize what's important first and find ways to eliminate those expenses that aren't so important.

December 3
Dreading Going Back to Work?

Then you could start off part time and use that as an opportunity to slowly get back into the pace. Alternatively think about other ways to earn an income such as turning your skills into an online business. This gives you the flexibility to set your own hours and work alongside your little ones.

December 4
Ignore the Mom Guilt

Feeling that mom-guilt of going back to work and leaving your child at daycare? Well if it wasn't important for you and your kids I'm sure you won't bother going back to work right? So when you are feeling guilty, think about why you made that decision to go back to work in the first place.

And most importantly remove yourself from any environment or person that tries to make you feel guilty about your decisions to go back to work. If anything, be proud and confident in your decision to support your family. Plus leaving the house and mingling with other adults can be good for your sanity.

December 5
Look into Flexible Offers

As a mother it helps to have a job that comes with flexible hours that can allow you to navigate things around your lifestyle. So when applying for jobs, be sure to check if they offer flexible hours or better still ask your current employer if more flexible hours could be offered.

That way if your child is sick or has an appointment, you won't feel under pressure about not showing up to work at a particular time. You can simply make up the hours as you go.

December 6
Plan in Advance

As a working mother, there's nothing more stressful in the morning than those school runs, especially if doing it yourself. One thing that can help minimize this is to prepare what you can the night before. This could be; your work outfit, the kids bags or even the ingredients you need to make breakfast. Doing this will save you so much time and stress the morning after.

December 7
Money Problems?

Finances becoming a strain? Perhaps you were that independent lady who made her own money before motherhood hit. And now you find yourself having to depend on a partner for financial support.

This can be extremely frustrating especially for someone who wasn't in the habit of relying on others for support. Know that you are now in a different phase in your life and as long as your other half is happy to support you financially, you have nothing to worry about. After all, being a mother is more than a full time job and you deserve all the support you can possibly get.

December 8
Find Time to Bond

As working mothers, you will be spending most of your hours at work. This can mean you don't get to see your little one(s) or spend enough time with them during the day. So when you do have the time with them, try to make the most of it.

Bonding time does not need to be hours. In fact whilst dropping/picking them from school, giving them bath times and reading them books to sleep, you could spend time engaging and bonding with them.

December 9
Track those Expenses

Write down your expenses. Do not lie to yourself. There is nothing like seeing it in black and white (or red). Keep track of your expenses on a spreadsheet or if you prefer, in a notebook.

It gives you a concrete idea of where you are spending too much and where you are spending too little. Do you really need to spend $5 a day on that coffee? That amounts to $1800 dollars a year just on your morning cup of coffee. Is it paramount to have the latest car every single year when you are hip deep in auto loans? Doing so will help you cut back unnecessary expenses and reduce financial pressures.

December 10
Positive Affirmation of the Day

Today is a day of positive affirmation. As you go through this day, repeat these words to yourself.

"I am filled with gratitude and joy, and I love that more and more money is flowing to me daily".

December 11
Watch Your Spending

Instead of selecting the first brand-name product you see, take the time to check what exactly you are getting. For example, many commercially branded cereal and grain products have exactly the same nutritional content as their generic cousins, at almost twice the price. You are really paying more for a brand name than the product itself.

December 12
Cut Those Credit Cards

The average person owns at least four cards, when realistically you only need one or two. One well-managed card does more for your credit score than the dozen overextended cards you have. If you can manage without one, why not cut them all?

Your credit score is not just affected by cards, but by other loans you have in your name, like your mortgage or auto loan.

December 13
Buy in Bulk

A great way to cut down your spending is to buy food in bulk, especially food that can be preserved in the fridge and freezer for longer. If buying perishable foods, you can prepare them in advance and preserve them in the refrigerator for later use.

Not only is this going to save you time having to cook every single day but will save you money on fast food and those quick takeaways. You can bulk shop during the weekends or on days you aren't working.

Alternatively, you can order your groceries online and have them delivered to your door to save you the extra stress of dashing off to the supermarket after a long tiring day.

December 14
Mind Your Company

You want to find a place to socialize where the people there are successful. This will present you with opportunities to meet new people with positive lifestyles. It will also open new opportunities by means of creating new contacts for you or new ways to build a financial abundance.

December 15
The Power of Spreadsheets

Spreadsheets can be an excellent way of managing finances. One advantage for choosing this method is the fact that you do not have to pay someone else to track your finances. You need to be aware of the fact that keeping track of all of your expenses and financial goals is not a quick and easy process. Once this spreadsheet is completed it should be put in a place where you will see it many times during the day.

Doing this will help you realize how much money you are spending, how long it will take you to reach your goal of financial abundance, and it will show you any unnecessary spending that you are doing.

December 16
Avoid Negative Thinking

Another important step in achieving financial abundance is to stop your negative thought processes. Ask yourself, do you really think making negative comments about yourself or your circumstances is going to make things better?

If you constantly sit around and think that something is too hard to do, in the end you will mentally trick yourself into believing this. On the contrary, if you tell yourself that a task will be easy to tackle, it will likely not present a challenge for you.

December 17
Know Your Expenses

One great way to manage your finances is to figure out what your monthly expenses are. It will be impossible to build wealth if you are spending more money on expenses than you are bringing in.

It doesn't matter what you do, all expenses need to be accounted for, down to the paper clips and staples. This will help you determine if your current set of circumstances will benefit or hinder your journey to financial abundance.

December 18
Family & Friend Support

Most challenges in life are made much easier with the support of family and friends. The challenges of managing money are no different. Your family and friends can help you to stay on track and remain motivated.

They can also offer an outside view of your situation and offer valuable insight that you may not have thought of on your own. Your family and friends will be more likely to hold you accountable when you do not stick to your financial goals than you will for yourself.

December 19
Positive Affirmation of the Day

Today is a day of positive affirmation. As you go through this day, repeat these words to yourself.

"I release all my negative thoughts about money and allow financial abundance to enter my life".

December 20
Create Passive Income

The beauty about passive income is the fact that you do not always need to be physically present to make your business work - which is the perfect way to make money for mothers. You could literally be at home cleaning after the kids or playing with them whilst your business is running itself in the background. Passive income can come in different forms - from renting from property, selling online courses, selling books on amazon, dropshipping and many others.

December 21
Other Income Opportunities

Generating income does not only have to involve going back to a full time job. Why not create a business instead? Why not seek alternative ways to boost your income? There are so many businesses you can start these days with little to no money, especially online. *(See glossary for some online business ideas)*

December 22
Inspirational Pictures

Using inspirational pictures can be quite helpful. Try hanging a few of them around the house where they will be seen often. This is a great way to visualize the things you wish to accomplish and stay motivated towards reaching your financial goals.

December 23
Check Your Income

One good question to ask yourself is, am I making enough money? Although it may be hard, if you are not making enough money, you may have to give up some things. You will be surprised by how much of a difference you can make by choosing to make your own coffee in the morning rather than buy a £4.99 Starbucks coffee.

If you analyze your current set of financial circumstances and come to the realization that you are not making enough money, it is definitely time to do something about it! Living within your means can help you minimize the financial strain and pressures.

December 24
Get Some Help

If you find yourself struggling to keep track of your finances yourself, a personal accountant can be very useful. Their purpose is to track all of your expenses and earnings. They can also be asked for expert advice about how you can further enlarge your earning potential. Personal accountants can also serve as a safety net when making purchases because you can ask them if the purchase fits your goals for your finances as well as your current financial situation.

December 25
Merry Christmas

Hey mama, just want to wish you a merry christmas today as you spend time with your family and loved ones. Take the time to relax and enjoy the day.

December 26
Positive Affirmation of the Day

Today is a day of positive affirmation. As you go through this day, repeat these words to yourself.

"I deserve to be prosperous and to have an abundance of money in my bank account".

December 27
Start that Business

There is no better way to make money than investing it and getting a return on investment. So rather than have £100 sitting in your savings account yielding you nothing, you could actually invest it in a business and make 10X that amount back. Gone are the days where you needed to invest thousands of dollars to start your business. These days, with the internet and a phone you could literally be on your way to starting your online business.

Starting an online business also gives you the opportunity to work from home, be your own boss and set your own hours - which is a great way to make extra income as a mother. Visit www.startupreine.com for online business ideas you can start today.

December 28
Get Organized

Keeping your surroundings free from clutter can help you stay organized with your finances. You may want to find ways of organizing things so that it becomes easier to track and manage your finances. So make sure those receipts, letters and bank statements are well organised in a place where you can easily find them so it becomes easier to track everything properly.

December 29
Examine Yourself

One way to keep track of finances is by analyzing your attitude towards spending money. By understanding your spending habits, it becomes easier to identify areas you need to work on.

When we are single, it is easy to splurge on certain things we consider as priority. However these priorities change once we become mothers and we must accept this and prioritize these new spending habits.

December 30
Look Into Investing

Sometimes it's impossible to eliminate things on our expense list. So what happens when you aren't making enough and everything seems to be a priority? You find ways to invest.

Investing your money can be a great way to make some extra money to cover up for those additional expenses.

Fortunately you do not need a lot of money to invest these days thanks to the internet. You could invest as little as $100 in an online business and make so much back. You could also look into other options like property, stock market, etc. So find ways to invest so you can generate additional income for yourself and your family.

(Visit www.startupreine.com for online business ideas you can invest on today)

December 31
Positive Affirmation of the Day

As you spend the last day of another eventful year, there's no better way to close things off than with another positive affirmation. So remember this as you step into another incredible new year.

"I attract health, money and happiness with ease, and I now have better health, more wealth and will become the happiest mother I can possibly be".

WIN THE MAMA TIME MUG

As a thank you for purchasing and reading this book, I am pleased to offer you the opportunity to WIN OUR Mama Time Mug. To WIN this mug simply follow the 2 steps below;

1. Leave a Review of this Book on Amazon

2. Screenshot your review and email to admin@seuletym.com

You will then be contacted with more instructions to WIN your free mug.

*PLEASE NOTE: *Only verified purchase reviews will qualify.*

The End

Printed in Great Britain
by Amazon

34932084R00184